Unit 1 Argumentative Essay
Relationships

STEP 1 ANALYZE THE MODEL

Is it better to be at the center of one group of friends or at the perimeter of several?

Read Source Materials

STEP 2 PRACTICE THE TASK

Is reaching consensus always a good idea, or are there times when it is better to disagree?

Read Source Materials

Write an Argumentative Essay

STEP 3 PERFORM THE TASK

Can you make real friends on the Internet?

Read Source Materials

Write an Argumentative Essay

Unit 2 Informative Essay
Ancient Civilizations

STEP 1 ANALYZE THE MODEL

Exploring Peru

Read Source Materials

STEP 2 PRACTICE THE TASK

In what ways are the Mayan and Egyptian pyramids alike and different?

Read Source Materials

Write a Comparison/Contrast Essay

STEP 3 PERFORM THE TASK

In what ways were the Maya, the Aztecs, and the Inca advanced for their time?

Read Source Materials

Write an Informative Esssay

Unit 3 Literary Analysis
Changes

© Houghton Mifflin Harcourt Publishing Company • Image Credits: ©Jill Stephenson/Alamy; ©Thomas Marchessault/Cutcaster; ©Orhan Cam/SuperStock

Unit 4 Mixed Practice
On Your Own

Relationships

Argumentative Essay

1 ANALYZE THE MODEL

Evaluate an argumentative essay about whether it is better to have many friends or a few close friends.

2 PRACTICE THE TASK

Write an argumentative essay that evaluates the benefits and drawbacks of reaching a consensus.

3 PERFORM THE TASK

Write an argumentative essay that offers reasons for or against making friends on the Internet.

Questioning another person's point of view is something we as humans love to do. Interacting with others—friends, neighbors, relatives, strangers—sometimes can lead to disagreements. Arguing, giving your reasons for your stance on an issue, and explaining your point of view, can be challenging on a person-to-person level.

The argumentative essay, on the other hand, is a more formally constructed argument.

IN THIS UNIT, you will learn how to write an argumentative essay that is based on your close reading and analysis of several relevant sources. You will learn a step-by-step approach to stating a claim—and then organizing your essay to support your claim in a clear and logical way.

Is it better to be at the center of one group of friends or at the perimeter of several?

You will read:

▶ **TWO INFORMATIONAL ARTICLES**
New School, New Groups of Friends

Teen Friendships: A Cauldron of Closeness

You will analyze:

▶ **A STUDENT MODEL**
Are Close Friends Better?

Source Materials for Step 1

The following texts were used by Ms. Jefferson's student, Philip Patel, as sources for his essay, "Are Close Friends Better than Many Friends?" As you read, make notes in the side columns and underline information that you find useful.

NOTES

New School, New Groups of Friends

It was really tough moving and starting from scratch at a new school, but after a year, I can say that there have been some good things as well as bad ones.

At my old school, I was part of a small group of "band geeks." That's what we called ourselves because that's what we were. I was right at the center of the group. I helped decide things like what we were going to do for fun, where we would sit in the lunchroom, and who we would hang out with. I'm not saying we were a clique but we knew each other really well and all agreed that we didn't want a lot of random kids hanging out with us.

The problem with a group like that is that it is hard to change and try new things without your friends getting mad at you or thinking you are rejecting them. So, at my new school, I've made an effort not to get too tight with any one group, but to try new things and stay flexible. I like being involved with a few groups and getting to know kids with different interests, even if I'm not right at the center of things. It's a relief not to have to worry about any of the intense friendship drama and just have fun doing cool activities and meeting new people.

I certainly miss my old gang of friends, but it's been a lot of fun having this chance to spread myself out.

Teen Friendships:
A CAULDRON OF CLOSENESS

NOTES

It will come as no surprise to parents that the teenage years are particularly intense ones when it comes to friendships and group dynamics. Many of our children find themselves both benefitting from—and sometimes struggling with—issues relating to being part of a group of friends.

Being part of a small, tight group can bolster a teen's sense of identity, supply a feeling of belonging, and provide close, loyal, and lasting friendships. Being part of a group can mean fewer awkward social moments, fewer social decisions to make, and more social stability and security.

Problems arise when a group becomes too small, too closed and limiting, or too controlling. The teenage years are times of great change and growth, and children should be free to rethink themselves and their friendships without the limitation of what can amount to a group veto.

Being the center of a tightly knit group can mean that there is less freedom to explore, meet new friends, and try out other interests and ideas. It is important that children understand that even the best of friends sometimes grow apart. They may no longer share the same interests. It is normal, natural, and healthy to change and grow, and even sometimes grow apart.

Maintaining a variety of friendships, some close, and some more casual, can help a teen through a tough transition out of a group. Also, it is important to remind teens to conduct themselves in a manner that they will have no cause to regret later on, always being fair, upfront, and generous. People of all ages do well when they remember that being right isn't as important as being kind.

Discuss and Decide

You have read two sources about social circles. Without going any further, discuss the question: Is it better to be at the center of one group of friends or at the perimeter of several? Cite text evidence in your discussion.

Analyze a Student Model for Step 1

Read Philip's essay closely. The red side notes are the comments that his teacher, Ms. Jefferson, wrote.

Philip Patel
Ms. Jefferson
English 9
November 18

Are Close Friends Better?

Interesting hook.

Do I really have to choose? If I could have my way, I would have both. I'd be at the center of a small group of close friends, but I'd also have a wide range of more casual friendships. Being at the perimeter of a number of groups would be a good balance to my more intense and cliquish small group. I'd have depth as well as breadth, and I'd have options if anything ever went wrong in my small group.

The issue and your claim are clear.

But let's say I can't have both and I have to choose one. In that case, I would choose to be at the center of a group of friends, even if that group were only three or four people. Here's why: no number of casual friends can equal the benefit of having one or two true close friends. Close friends are nothing like casual friends. You can trust them. You can laugh with them. They are there for you when life is good and when it is tough.

Good transition.

Valid reason, clearly stated.

Also, being at the center of something is completely different from being on the outside. When you are in the center of a small group of friends, you have a say over things. You can say what you prefer and what you really think. You can make decisions, or help make decisions. You are in charge.

Excellent point.

When you are on the perimeter of a group, you are on the outside looking in. You can decide to join in or not, but you can't really participate in decision-making, and that can get frustrating.

Valid opposing claim.

It is nice to know people from many different groups with many different interests, but if none of them are close friends, then you are still missing out.

It's true that being at the center of a small group is like putting all your eggs in one basket. Yes, it has more risks, but it also has more rewards. There is nothing quite as special as a group of close friends.

Concluding statement is well made.

Well done!

Discuss and Decide

Did Philip's essay convince you that it is better to have a small circle of friends?
If so, which of his reasons are the most compelling?

Terminology of Argumentative Texts

Read each term and explanation. Then look back at Philip Patel's argumentative essay and find an example to complete the chart.

Term	Explanation	Example from Philip's Essay
audience	The **audience** for your argument is a group of people that you want to convince. As you develop your argument, consider your audience's knowledge level and concerns.	
purpose	The **purpose** for writing an argument is to sway the audience. Your purpose should be clear, whether it is to persuade your audience to agree with your claim, or to motivate your audience to take some action.	
precise claim	A **precise claim** confidently states your viewpoint. Remember that you must be able to find reasons and evidence to support your claim, and that you must distinguish your claim from opposing claims.	
reason	A **reason** is a statement that supports your claim. (You should have more than one reason.) Note that you will need to supply evidence for each reason you state.	
opposing claim	An **opposing claim,** or **counterclaim,** shares the point of view of people who do not agree with your claim. Opposing claims must be fairly presented with evidence.	

Is reaching consensus always a good idea, or are there times when it is better to disagree?

You will read:

▶ **A NEWSPAPER ARTICLE**
Consensus Will Be Used to Decide School Board Policy

▶ **AN INFORMATIONAL ARTICLE**
How to Reach a Consensus

▶ **A LIST**
Is Consensus Decision-Making Right for Your Group?

▶ **TWO LETTERS TO THE EDITOR**

You will write:

▶ **AN ARGUMENTATIVE ESSAY**
Is reaching a consensus always a good idea, or are there times when it is better to disagree?

Source Materials for Step 2

AS YOU READ Analyze and annotate the sources in ways that help you reach a decision regarding consensus.

Source 1: Newspaper Article

Consensus Will Be Used to Decide School Board Policy

by Soledad Stephens, Education Correspondent   May 25, 2012

At a meeting last night, the Tiberi Township School Board chose a new method to determine standards for grade promotion. Normally the 12-person board votes on the proposals. Now they will use consensus to build a plan of action acceptable to all. Although none are likely to get their first choice, there will also be no winners and no losers.

Consensus decision-making is very different from voting. Voting is a way to choose between alternatives. With consensus, a group can bring the best parts of many proposals together to create something new. Voting is faster, but it may leave some "defeated" voters upset with the outcome. When a group achieves consensus after a thorough discussion, all parties are on board with the outcome.

"I'm just pleased we will be working together to shape a proposal that everyone can

get behind," said School Board President Patti Rincon.

However, not all are in consensus about using consensus.

"Consensus is too much compromise," said parent Tyrell Washington. "Everyone gives up something and no one really likes the final result. They should keep working until they have a proposal that everyone likes, unanimously!"

School administrator Jesse VanDeLaar thinks just the opposite. "These decisions should be made by the experts," he declared. "It really isn't useful to vote or reach consensus. This is not a popularity contest—it's a question of what the research has shown will or will not work."

Good luck to the members of the school board on reaching a consensus that will be accepted by all stakeholders—parents, teachers, *and* school administrators.

How to Reach a Consensus

A *consensus* is when a group of people reaches a general agreement. Getting to a consensus requires a special decision-making process that takes everyone's opinions and concerns into account. In consensus decision-making, everyone is included, everyone participates, everyone's voice is equal, and everyone works towards the same goal—finding a solution.

1 Define and describe the issue that needs to be decided.

2 Decide how your group will reach a final decision. (Some groups insist on unanimity; others accept a consensus with one or two dissenting voices.)

3 List all the concerns that the final proposal should address.

4 Brainstorm and record a list of possible solutions. Encourage every participant to offer ideas, opinions, and comments.

5 Evaluate the list of alternatives. Write up a draft proposal that combines the best of all the ideas.

6 Revise the proposal until it best meets the interests of the group.

Close Read

You've read two sources on reaching a consensus. Explain some advantages to making decisions this way, and cite text evidence to support your response.

_____

_____

Is Consensus Decision-Making Right for Your Group?

Advantages of Consensus Decision Making:

▶ Consensus decision-making helps build trust and a sense of community.

▶ Everyone's ideas are included, which leads to a wider range of possible solutions.

▶ The solutions are supported by the whole group.

Reaching a consensus may be difficult if:

▶ the group has not worked together before or is too large (15 or more).

▶ some members do not understand or accept the consensus-seeking process, or argue, bully, or intimidate others.

▶ the issue is complicated with few viable solutions available.

▶ one member has more power than others (this may discourage others from speaking freely).

▶ there is a lack or trust among group members.

▶ there is not enough time for discussion.

▶ group leaders try to control outcomes rather than facilitate discussion.

▶ one or two "dissenters" hold up the whole process.

▶ there is no agreed-upon consensus process for the group to use.

Discuss and Decide

When might making a decision by consensus not be the best method to use?

1. Analyze   2. Practice   3. Perform

Source 4: Letters to the Editor

To the Editor

I'm writing to protest the School Board's recent adoption of the consensus decision-making method to decide grade promotion policy. This is not a situation where it is appropriate to choose a course of action by finding something that everyone can agree on. Maybe everyone agrees on a plan that makes no sense at all. Decisions about grade promotions should be made by administrators who have responsibility and experts who have special knowledge. We owe our students the BEST decisions, not just the most popular ones.

Yours truly,
Jesse VanDeLaar
Deputy Principal

To the Editor

Congratulations to the School Board for choosing to make their policy decisions by consensus! No longer will the policies they adopt be the subject of bitter disagreements and lackluster support. We parents will no longer feel like cats who have left the mice to play. When the whole school board unites behind a plan, then teachers, parents, and students will unite behind it as well. A plan which has taken into consideration the opinions and interests of all the members—and survived extensive debate—is a plan that will stand the test of time.

In a world with far too much strife and conflict, few leaders seem to have the skills needed to compromise and work together effectively. Hats off to the school board for leading by example.

Mary Anne Dunlop
Parent

Discuss and Decide

Which claims in one letter are not directly refuted in the other letter?

Respond to Questions on Step 2 Sources

These questions will help you analyze the sources you've read. Use your notes and refer back to the sources in order to answer the questions. Your answers to these questions will help you write your essay.

1 Evaluate the sources. Is the evidence from one source more credible than the evidence from another source? When you evaluate the credibility of a source, examine the expertise of the author and/or the organization responsible for the information. Record your reasons in the chart.

Source	Credible?	Reasons
Newspaper Article Consensus Will Be Used to Decide School Board Policy		
Informational Article How to Reach a Consensus		
List Is Consensus Decision-Making Right for Your Group?		
Letters to the Editor		

2 **Prose Constructed-Response** If you disagreed with Mary Anne Dunlop's position on decision-making by consensus, which sources would you use to refute her argument? Why?

_____

_____

3 **Prose Constructed-Response** Which source best complements the information found in the list, "Is Consensus Decision-Making Right for Your Group?" Explain your rationale, citing evidence from the text.

_____

_____

Searching for Evidence

Every reason you offer to support the central claim of your argument must be upheld by evidence. It is useful to think ahead about evidence when you are preparing to write an argument. If there is no evidence to support your claim, you will need to revise your claim. The evidence you provide must be relevant, or related to your claim. It must also be sufficient. Sufficient evidence is both clear and varied.

Use this chart to help you vary the types of evidence you provide to support your reasons.

Types of Evidence	What Does It Look Like?
Anecdotes: personal examples or stories that illustrate a point	**Letters to the Editor** "No longer will the policies they adopt be the subject of bitter disagreements and lackluster support."
Commonly accepted beliefs: ideas that most people share	**Newspaper Article** "'Consensus is too much compromise,' said parent Tyrell Washington."
Examples: specific instances or illustrations of a general idea	**Newspaper Article** "Normally the 12-person board votes on the proposals. Now they will use consensus to build a plan of action acceptable to all."
Expert opinion: statement made by an authority on the subject	**Newspaper Article** "'. . . we will be working together to shape a proposal that everyone can get behind,' said School Board President Patti Rincon."
Facts: statements that can be proven true, such as statistics or other numerical information	**Informational Article** "A *consensus* is when a group of people reaches a general agreement."

ASSIGNMENT

Write an argumentative essay to answer the question: Is reaching consensus always a good idea? Are there times when it is better to disagree?

Planning and Prewriting

Before you draft your essay, complete some important planning steps.

Claim ➡ Reasons ➡ Evidence

 You may prefer to do your planning on a computer.

Make a Precise Claim

1. Is reaching consensus always a good idea? Are there times when it is better to disagree?   yes ☐   no ☐

2. Review the evidence on pages 10–13. Do the sources support your position?   yes ☐   no ☐

3. If you answered *no* to Question 2, you can either change your position or do additional research to find supporting evidence.

4. State your claim. It should be precise. It should contain the issue and your position on the issue.

Issue: Decision-making by consensus

Your position on the issue: _____

Your precise claim: _____

State Reasons

Next gather support for your claim. Identify several valid reasons that justify your position.

Reason 1	Reason 2	Reason 3

Find Evidence

You have identified reasons that support your claim. Summarize your reasons in the chart below. Then complete the chart by identifying evidence that supports your reasons.

Relevant Evidence: The evidence you plan to use must be *relevant* to your argument. That is, it should directly and factually support your position.

Sufficient Evidence: Additionally, your evidence must be *sufficient* to make your case. That is, you need to supply enough evidence to convince others

Short Summary of Reasons	Evidence
Reason 1	Relevant? _____ Sufficient? _____
Reason 2	Relevant? _____ Sufficient? _____
Reason 3	Relevant? _____ Sufficient? _____

Finalize Your Plan

Whether you are writing your essay at home or working in a timed situation at school, it is important to have a plan. You will save time and create a more organized, logical essay by planning the structure before you start writing.

Use your responses on pages 16–17, as well as your close reading notes, to complete the graphic organizer.

▶ Think about how you will grab your reader's attention with an interesting fact or anecdote.

▶ Identify the issue and your position.

▶ State your precise claim.
▶ List the likely opposing claim and how you will counter it.

▶ Restate your claim.

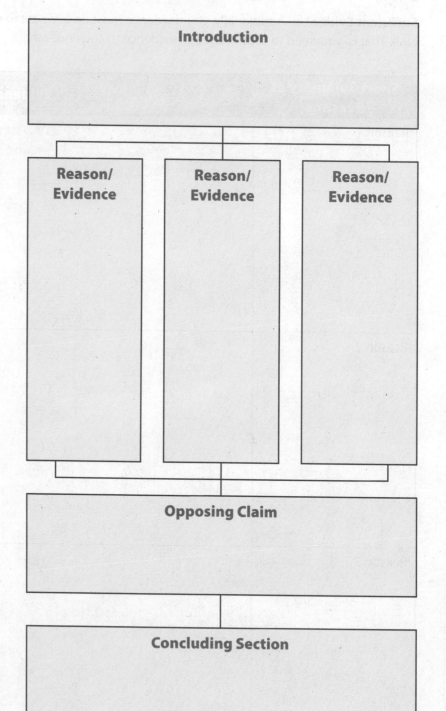

Introduction

Reason/ Evidence   **Reason/ Evidence**   **Reason/ Evidence**

Opposing Claim

Concluding Section

Draft Your Essay

As you write, think about:

▶ **Audience:** Your teacher

▶ **Purpose:** Demonstrate your understanding of the specific requirements of an argumentative essay.

▶ **Style:** Use a formal and objective tone that isn't defensive.

▶ **Transitions:** Use words, such as *furthermore* or *another reason,* to create cohesion or flow.

Revise

Revision Checklist: Self Evaluation

Use the checklist below to guide your analysis.

 If you drafted your essay on the computer, you may wish to print it out so that you can more easily evaluate it.

Ask Yourself	Tips	Revision Strategies
Does the introduction grab the audience's attention and include a precise claim?	Draw a wavy line under the attention-grabbing text. Bracket the claim.	Add an attention grabber. Add a claim or rework the existing one to make it more precise.
Do at least two valid reasons support the claim? Is each reason supported by relevant and sufficient evidence?	Underline each reason. Circle each piece of evidence, and draw an arrow to the reason it supports.	Add reasons or revise existing ones to make them more valid. Add relevant evidence to ensure that your support is sufficient.
Do transitions create cohesion and link related parts of the argument?	Put a star next to each transition.	Add words, phrases, or clauses to connect related ideas that lack transitions.
Are the reasons in the order that is most persuasive?	Number the reasons in the margin, ranking them by their strength and effectiveness.	Rearrange the reasons into a more logical order of importance.
Are opposing claims fairly acknowledged and refuted?	Put a plus sign by any sentence that addresses an opposing claim.	Add sentences that identify and address those opposing claims.
Does the concluding section restate the claim?	Put a box around the restatement of your claim.	Add a sentence that restates your claim.

Revision Checklist: Peer Review

Exchange your essay with a classmate, or read it aloud to your partner. As you read and comment on your classmate's essay, focus on logic, organization, and evidence—not on whether you agree with the author's claim. Help each other identify parts of the draft that need strengthening, reworking, or a new approach.

What To Look For	Notes for My Partner
Does the introduction grab the audience's attention and include a precise claim?	
Do at least two valid reasons support the claim? Is each reason supported by relevant and sufficient evidence?	
Do transitions create cohesion and link related parts of the argument?	
Are the reasons in the order that is most persuasive?	
Are opposing claims fairly acknowledged and refuted?	
Does the concluding section restate the claim?	

Edit

 Edit your essay to correct spelling, grammar, and punctuation errors.

PERFORM THE TASK

Can you make real friends on the Internet?

You will read:

▶ **A NEWSPAPER ARTICLE**
Study: The Internet Helps You Make More Friends, Be More Social

▶ **A BLOG**
Social Media, Pretend Friends, and the Lie of False Intimacy

▶ **A MAGAZINE ARTICLE**
Making Friends Through the Internet

You will write:

▶ **AN ARGUMENTATIVE ESSAY**
Can you make real friends on the Internet?

Study:
The Internet Helps You Make More Friends, Be More Social

by Graeme McMillan, June 16, 2011

AS YOU READ *Analyze the data presented in the articles. Look for evidence that supports your position that you can make real friends online, or inspires you to change your position.*

NOTES

It's the kind of news you can use next time concerned parents bring up the idea that the internet is making people more withdrawn and closed off from the rest of humanity: A new study from the Pew Research Center has found that online social networks actually seem to make people more social.

Pew polled 2,255 Americans during October and November last year, and of the 1,787 internet users in that group, 47% used social networking sites. Facebook was used by 92% of the 975 people that used social networks, with MySpace in second place, with 29%.

10 Linkedin and Twitter trailed behind, with 18% and 13% respectively.

That's almost twice as many as in 2008, when the survey was last held. But more interestingly, there's also been a rise in the number of close friendships people are reporting when compared with 2008—2.16 close friends on average, compared with 2008's 1.93—with that increase being lead by those online, who reported an average of 2.26 close friends to the offline respondents' 1.75. It gets even better when you look at those using social networks, who reported 2.45 close friends on average.

Discuss and Decide

The author includes information about the number of close friends reported. What trend does the Pew Survey seem to reveal? Cite text evidence in your discussion.

> _...online Americans tend to have 664 [social] ties on average, compared with an offline average of around 506._

The study even looked into the number of social ties internet
20 users and non-internet users have, and found that online Americans
tend to have 664 ties on average, compared with an offline average
of around 506. That number goes crazy when you start to plug in
different social networks, however: Facebook users average 648 social
ties, but Twitter users have an average of 838.

So, the next time someone says that they think the internet is bad
for society, the answer is clear: Sign them up for Twitter, and see how
they feel a couple of weeks later.

© Houghton Mifflin Harcourt Publishing Company

NOTES

Close Read

1. How did Pew Research collect their data?

_____

_____

2. Explain the change in the number of people using social networking sites from 2008 to 2011.

_____

3. Are the increases in "close friends" and "ties" similar or different? Cite evidence from the text to support your answer.

_____

_____

_____

Social Media, Pretend Friends, and the Lie of False Intimacy

AS YOU READ *Note all the issues that having many online friends can create. Is your opinion altered by this information?*

NOTES

It's not an illusion. We really are doing more with each 24 hours, as technology enables (or forces) us to interact and intersect and do and consume with unprecedented volume and vigor. **We live our lives at breakneck speed because we can, because we feel we have to keep up, and because every macro and micro breeze blows in that direction.**

I remember the days before social media when I would get 20 phone calls per day and 50 or 60 emails, and felt exhausted by the pace of communication. Now we've traded the telephone for other connection points (I only get 2-3 calls per day), but the overall number of people ringing our doorbell through some mechanism has ballooned like Charles Barkley.

The number of "inboxes" we possess is staggering: Email (3 accounts for me), public Twitter, Twitter DM, public Facebook, Facebook messages, Facebook chat, Linkedin messages, public Google +, Google + messages, blog comments, Skype, text messages, Instagram, phone, voice mail, and several topically or geographically specific forums, groups and social networks. That's a lot of relationship bait in the water.

Close Read

Which specific words does the author use in the text to suggest his or her position? What inference can you make about the nature of this position?

_____

_____

The Lie of Opportunity

How do we justify this? How do we convince ourselves that slicing our attention so thin the turkey becomes translucent is a good idea?

We do it because we believe that more relationships provides more opportunity.

"It's not what you know, it's who you know."

"Social media makes a big world smaller."

"Linkedin is for people you know, Facebook is for people you used to know, Twitter is for people you want to know."

30   All of these chestnuts are passed around like a flu strain because they make intuitive sense. But common among them is the **underlying premise that interacting with more people is inherently better than interacting with fewer people.** I have always believed this to be true, and in fact have delivered the lines above in presentations and on this blog. But today, I'm no longer convinced.

Instead I wonder, what if we have it ALL wrong?

I recognize this is not purely an either/or scenario, and relationships that began with a Twitter exchange or series of blog comments can flourish into treasured real-world ties.

40   But those situations where we "meet" someone through social media, have the opportunity to interact in real life, and then develop a relationship that creates true friendship are few and far between. **And as social media gets bigger and more pervasive, this chasm becomes even more difficult to cross.** As my own networks in social media have gotten larger, I've ended up talking about my personal life less, because a large percentage of that group don't know me, or my wife, or my kids, or my town, or my interests. I don't want to bore people with the inanities of the everyday. (Facebook is the one exception, as I've always kept my personal account relatively small).

50   To some degree, I think this explains the popularity of Google + among people with very large followings on Twitter and/or Facebook. Google + provides a chance for a do-over, to create a new group of connections that are more carefully cultivated.

But that's just medicating the symptoms, not curing the disease. **Fundamentally, technology and our use of it isn't—as we've all hoped—bringing us closer together.** In fact, it may be driving us farther apart, as we know more and more people, but know less and less about each of them.

Making Friends Out of Connections

60 **Maybe we should be focused less on making a lot of connections, and focused more on making a few real friends?** I'm going to try to work on this, to identify people with whom I want to develop real friendships, and make a concerted effort to do so, even if it means answering fewer tweets and blog comments from a much larger group of casual connections.

We have to take at least some of these social media spawned relationships to the next level, otherwise what's the point beyond generating clicks and newsletter subscribers?

You think you know someone, but you don't. And that's social
70 **media's fault. But more so, our own.**

Close Read

What claim and counterclaim about the value of Internet contacts does the blogger make? Be sure to cite textual evidence in your response.

_____

_____

_____

1. Analyze   2. Practice   3. Perform

Making Friends Through The Internet
Advantages and disadvantages of meeting friends online
by Sally Arthur

Meeting friends on the Internet can have its advantages and disadvantages. There are a number of factors to consider.

Meeting friends online can happen more quickly than it might happen offline. You can even become friends with someone who lives in a different part of the world.

You can remain anonymous on the Internet. You do not have to share information about where you live, how old you are, or any personal details about your life. Online, you can be whoever you want to be, or just be yourself. This allows people to practice their
10 social skills in an anonymous setting.

One major disadvantage of making friends online is that you do not always know if people are who they say they are. Just as it can be a good thing to be anonymous to protect your safety and personal information, anonymity can be dangerous, too. If you are dealing with someone who is not forthcoming about their identity, you don't know his or her motive for doing so.

Making friends online also may prevent people from socializing outside of the Internet. While having friends online is a good way to find people with similar interests, friends who exist only on a
20 computer screen do not provide the companionship necessary to sustain friendships. If having Internet friends comes at the cost of neglecting friends offline, the Internet becomes a disadvantage.

While there are advantages and disadvantages to meeting friends online, it is up to every individual to use discretion and be safe.

NOTES

Discuss and Decide

Reviewing the advantages and disadvantages Arthur lists, do you have a sense of her bias? Explain your thinking, citing evidence from the text.

Respond to Questions on Step 3 Sources

These questions will help you analyze the sources you've read. Use your notes and refer back to the sources to answer the questions. Your answers to these questions will help you write your essay.

1 Is the evidence from one source more credible than the evidence from another source? When you evaluate the credibility of a source, examine the expertise of the author and/or the organization responsible for the information. Record your reasons.

Source	Credible?	Reasons
Newspaper Article Study: The Internet Helps You Make More Friends, Be More Social		
Blog Social Media, Pretend Friends, and the Lie of False Intimacy		
Magazine Article Making Friends Through the Internet		

2 **Prose Constructed-Response** What point about making friends online is raised in all three sources? Why is this point important to address when making an informed decision about the validity of online friendships? Support your answer with details and evidence.

_____

_____

_____

3 **Prose Constructed-Response** Does the evidence in "Making Friends Through the Internet" support or contradict the evidence in "Study: The Internet Helps You Make More Friends, Be More Social"? Use details from the article to support your answer.

_____

_____

_____

Part 2: Write

ASSIGNMENT

ASSIGNMENT

You have read about making friends online. Now write an argumentative essay explaining why you agree or disagree with the idea that you can make real friends on the Internet. Support your claim with details from what you have read.

Plan

Use the graphic organizer to help you outline the structure of your argumentative essay.

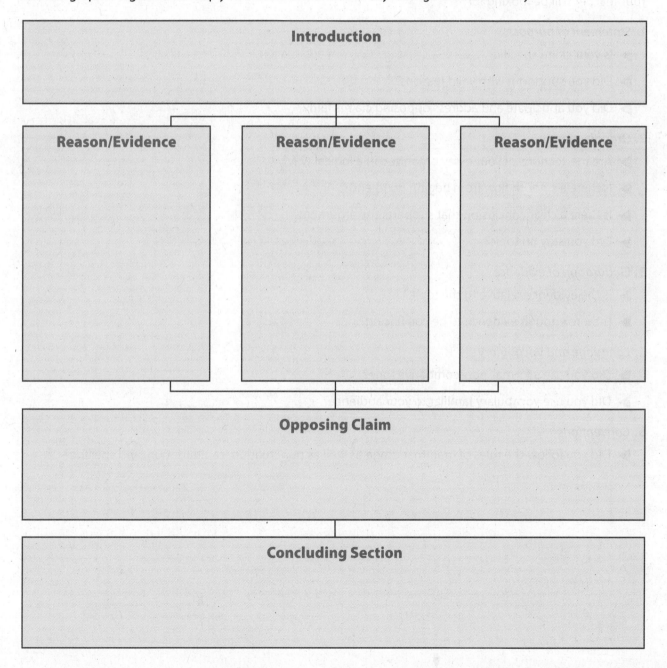

Introduction

Reason/Evidence

Reason/Evidence

Reason/Evidence

Opposing Claim

Concluding Section

Draft

 Use your notes and completed graphic organizer to write a first draft of your argumentative essay.

Revise and Edit

 Look back over your essay and compare it to the Evaluation Criteria. Revise your essay and edit it to correct spelling, grammar, and punctuation errors.

Evaluation Criteria

Your teacher will be looking for:

1. Statement of purpose

▶ Is your claim specific?

▶ Did you support it with valid reasons?

▶ Did you anticipate and address opposing claims fairly?

2. Organization

▶ Are the sections of your essay organized in a logical way?

▶ Is there a smooth flow from beginning to end?

▶ Is there a clear conclusion that supports the argument?

▶ Did you stay on topic?

3. Elaboration of evidence

▶ Is the evidence relative to the topic?

▶ Is there enough evidence to be convincing?

4. Language and Vocabulary

▶ Did you use a formal, non-combative tone?

▶ Did you use vocabulary familiar to your audience?

5. Conventions

▶ Did you follow the rules of grammar usage as well as punctuation, capitalization, and spelling?

Ancient Civilizations

Informative Essay

ANALYZE THE MODEL

Evaluate informative essays on Cuzco, Peru, and Machu Picchu.

PRACTICE THE TASK

Write a comparison/ contrast essay on how the Mayan and Egyptian pyramids are alike and different.

PERFORM THE TASK

Write an informative essay about the successes of the Maya, the Aztecs, and the Inca.

An informative essay, also called an expository essay, is a short work of nonfiction that informs and explains. Unlike fiction, nonfiction is mainly written to convey factual information, although writers of nonfiction shape information in a way that matches their own purposes. Nonfiction writing can be found in newspaper, magazine, and online articles, as well as in biographies, speeches, movie and book reviews, and true-life adventure stories.

The nonfiction topics that you will read about in this unit discuss real facts and events about ancient civilizations and structures.

IN THIS UNIT, you will analyze information from nonfiction articles, graphics, and data displays. You will study a variety of text structures that are frequently used in the writing of informative text. You will use these text structures to plan and write your essays.

Exploring Peru

You will read:

▶ **AN INSTRUCTIONAL ARTICLE**
Chart a Course That Works!

You will analyze:

▶ **TWO STUDENT MODELS**
Cuzco, Peru

Machu Picchu

Source Materials for Step 1

Ms. Margolis' students read the article below to help them learn strategies for structuring informative essays. As you read, underline information that you find useful.

Chart a Course That Works!

You probably have already had tough writing assignments that required you to plan, research, and write an informative essay. Whether the subject is science, history, or another nonfiction topic, you should decide in advance how you will structure your essay. Don't just start somewhere and keep on writing until you have met the page requirement. Structure first! What do I mean by structure? A structure is a system in which the parts all have a function. When you write an informative essay, each part should support your message. Graphic organizers can help you plan your organizational structure.

Main Idea and Supporting Details

The purpose of any informative essay is to give your reader more information about a topic, whether that be explaining a topic or describing a process. Use a graphic organizer like the one below to focus on your main idea and the details or descriptions to support it. Jot down your main idea or central point. Then identify the details you will use to support or explain your main idea. To keep on track, refer regularly to your graphic organizer as you write.

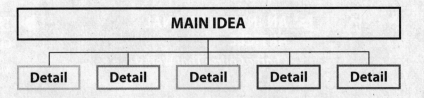

Developing Your Topic

Many scientific and historical essays revolve around cause-effect relationships. Sometimes multiple factors contribute to one event. Sometimes a single event can lead to multiple outcomes. In some situations, one event triggers the next event to happen, and that causes another event to occur.

1. Cause-to-Effect Organization

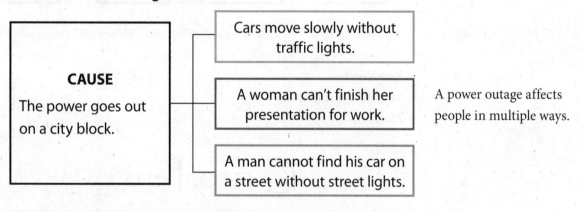

CAUSE
The power goes out on a city block.

Cars move slowly without traffic lights.

A woman can't finish her presentation for work.

A man cannot find his car on a street without street lights.

A power outage affects people in multiple ways.

2. Multiple-Causes Organization

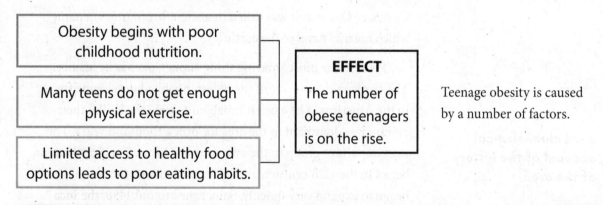

Obesity begins with poor childhood nutrition.

Many teens do not get enough physical exercise.

Limited access to healthy food options leads to poor eating habits.

EFFECT
The number of obese teenagers is on the rise.

Teenage obesity is caused by a number of factors.

3. Chronological Order

Events happen in chronological order, which means that one event follows another. There is a sequence of events that occur in time order.

First → **Then** → **Then** → **Finally**

Discuss and Decide

What are some events that can be told in chronological order?

Analyze Two Student Models for Step 1

Ken structured his informative essay topically, relating the main idea first, followed by its supporting details. Read his essay closely. The red side notes are comments made by his teacher, Ms. Margolis.

Ken's Model

```
         ┌─────────────────────────┐
         │        MAIN IDEA         │
         │  Cuzco is a unique city. │
         └─────────────────────────┘
              │      │      │      │
   ┌──────────┐ ┌──────────┐ ┌──────────┐ ┌──────────┐
   │ History  │ │Architecture│ │Festivals│ │Prestigious│
   │          │ │          │ │ & Food   │ │  Awards   │
   └──────────┘ └──────────┘ └──────────┘ └──────────┘
```

Ken Norris
Ms. Margolis, English
March 15

Cuzco, Peru

In southeastern Peru, nestled in the Andes at a height of 11,200 feet above sea level, is one of the world's most amazing cities. It's Cuzco, or *Qosqo* as it was called in ancient Incan times, a name which means "navel of the earth."

Perhaps the most amazing thing about Cuzco is its history. The city is said to be one of the oldest inhabited developments in the Americas. The earliest inhabitants were the Killki; their culture was dominant in the area for over a thousand years. The next important group in the area were the Incas. Their civilization began in the 12th century, and by the early 1400s the Inca Empire began to expand very quickly. Sometime around 1450, the inca (king) Pachacutec developed Cuzco into the capital of the empire. The city was designed in the shape of a puma, and two rivers were diverted with canals to prevent flooding. By 1500, Cuzco was one of the richest and most important cities in the Americas.

good chronological account of the history of the area

But then something new happened on the continent. Spanish conquistadors arrived. The Incas were involved in civil war, many fell victim to European diseases, and their warriors were no match for Spanish armored horseback cavalry. In 1533, a Spanish force of just 180 men under Francisco Pizarro took the city. Three years later, a force of between 10,000 and 100,000 Incas tried unsuccessfully to reclaim it. Cuzco remained under Spanish rule until 1821, when Peru declared independence.

One of the results of the Spanish conquest was the remarkable mix of architecture in Cuzco. The Inca stonework and precious metals were like nothing Spaniards had ever seen. Great blocks of stone were so accurately cut that there was no need for mortar. One such block that remains as part of a wall weighs over 30 tons. The Spanish took the precious metals, including 700 gold panels from the Qorikancha temple that each weighed nearly five pounds. They destroyed the Inca's religious and political buildings, but built their own churches and palaces on the Inca foundations. The city retains its Inca layout and numerous examples of both Inca stonework and Spanish baroque architecture.

very interesting to learn how the Spanish and Incan influences both remain in the city

A modern visitor to Cuzco will delight in the city's festivals, its indigenous foods (such as the famed "cuy," roasted guinea pig), its temples and palaces, and its sacred history.

Did the Spanish conquerors have an influence on these festivals?

For these and many other reasons, Cuzco is a most amazing city. It is no wonder that it has been called the archaeological capital of the Americas, has been named to UNESCO's Cultural Heritage List, and is also a World Heritage Site.

Discuss and Decide

Discuss at least two reasons why Cuzco is considered a World Heritage site. Cite text evidence in your discussion.

Claudia chose to use a chronological text structure for her essay. In this essay, Claudia describes the history of Machu Picchu, from its discovery to its classification as a World Heritage site. Ms. Margolis made her notes in red.

Claudia's Model

Machu Picchu's beginnings → Hiram Bingham and Machu Picchu → Location → Machu Picchu in the present

Claudia Zhang
Ms. Margolis, English
March 15

Machu Picchu

Machu Picchu's Beginnings

Machu Picchu, "The Lost City of the Incas," is the site of one of the most well-known set of ruins in the world. Historians believe that Machu Picchu was constructed during the height of the Inca Empire in the 15th century. About 100 years after it was built, Machu Picchu was abandoned, though historians are not sure of the exact reason why. The Spanish had arrived in South America around this time, so some consider this a possible explanation for its abandonment. However, there is no evidence that the Spanish ever entered Machu Picchu. Some historians believe a smallpox epidemic forced the Inca to leave Machu Picchu.

> *That is quite the mystery! Are there any other theories to account for its abandonment?*

Another mystery that surrounds Machu Picchu is what its purpose was. Some archaeologists believe that the city was a royal estate for Inca nobles and emperors. Other guesses have included a women's retreat, a city created solely for the coronation of kings, a prison, or a site for testing new crops. The belief that Machu Picchu might have been a religious site is supported by its geographic location, close to the mountains and other natural features that were important to the Inca.

Hiram Bingham and Machu Picchu

Hiram Bingham, an American archaeologist, was searching for the Incan city of Vilcabamba when he arrived at Machu Picchu in the summer of 1911. Bingham and his team of explorers walked on foot and traveled on mules to journey from Cuzco to the Urubamba Valley in Peru. A farmer told them of the ruins at the top of the mountain. On July 24, led by a small group of peasants and an 11-year-old boy, Bingham first saw Machu Picchu.

Bingham excavated artifacts from the site and brought them to Yale University. He also wrote a book called *The Lost City of the Incas* that prompted many eager tourists to travel to Peru and make the same journey Bingham had made along the Inca Trail. Machu Picchu was no longer known to just the local peasants, but had become a travel destination for the world.

In the history books, Bingham is listed as the person who made Machu Picchu known to the world, but it is believed that missionaries and other explorers had arrived at Machu Picchu in the 19th and early 20th centuries.

Location

Machu Picchu is located in the mountain forests of the Peruvian Andes. Terraces, walls, and stairways peek out from the sloping mountains, creating a sight that is beautiful to the eye. The Incas used stones to hammer the larger stones together snugly, without mortar.

The site has terraced fields and a complex irrigation system that would have been useful in the different sectors of the city, including a farming zone, a royal district, a sacred area, and a residential neighborhood.

Machu Picchu in the Present

In 2007, Machu Picchu was named one of the New Seven Wonders of the World. It is Peru's most visited site, as well as South America's most famous ruins. To protect the ruins and prevent mountainside erosion, the government has taken steps to ensure that tourists exercise proper care when visiting the site.

Think about including more detail in this paragraph: how long did the trip take?

I see why he wouldn't be named as the person to "discover" Machu Picchu, since it had never been lost!

The Inca were an advanced society. Strong facts support the theories you presented about the site's purpose.

Discuss and Decide

Why is Machu Picchu known as the "Lost City of the Incas"?

Terminology of Informative Essays

Read each term and explanation. Then look back and analyze each student model. Find an example to complete the chart.

Term	Explanation	Example from Student Essays
topic	The **topic** is a word or phrase that tells what the essay is about.	
text structure	The **text structure** is the organizational pattern of an essay.	
focus	The **focus** is the controlling, or overarching, idea that states the main point the writer chooses to make.	
supporting evidence	The **supporting evidence** is relevant quotations and concrete details that support the focus.	
domain-specific vocabulary	**Domain-specific vocabulary** is content-specific words that are not generally used in conversation.	
text features	**Text features** are design elements that help organize the text, such as headings, boldface type, italic type, bulleted or numbered lists, sidebars, and graphic aids including charts, tables, timelines, illustrations, and photographs.	

Prose Constructed-Reponse Which essay provided more details to support its main idea? Support your claim by citing text evidence.

_____

_____

_____

In what ways are the Mayan and Egyptian pyramids alike and different?

You will read:

▶ **A MAGAZINE ARTICLE**
The Pyramids of Giza

▶ **DATA ANALYSIS**
The Great Pyramid at Giza

▶ **A TRAVEL GUIDE**
Visiting the Mayan Pyramids

▶ **INFOGRAPHIC**
El Castillo Mayan Pyramid
The Great Pyramid at Giza

You will write:

▶ **A COMPARISON / CONTRAST ESSAY**
In what ways are the Mayan and Egyptian pyramids alike and different?

Source Materials for Step 2

AS YOU READ You will be writing a comparison-and-contrast essay about the Mayan and Egyptian pyramids. Carefully study the sources in Step 2. For each text, annotate by underlining and circling information that may be useful to you when you write your essay.

Source 1: Magazine Article

THE PYRAMIDS OF GIZA

by Helena Gustafson

When you hear the word *pyramids,* what picture do you see in your head? More likely than not, you see three magnificent stone structures rising out of the desert sands. These are the pyramids of Giza, Egypt, famous not only for their stupendous size and dramatic shape, but also for the astonishing skill with which they were built thousands of years ago.

The pyramids at Giza

1. Analyze   2. Practice   3. Perform

Silhouettes of the three largest pyramids at Giza: Menkaura, Khafra, and Khufu

The three pyramids at Giza were designed as monumental tombs for pharaohs (kings) of Egypt, to house their bodies after death and to help them achieve eternal life in the afterworld. Each was made by and for a different pharaoh: King Khufu built the Great Pyramid (the biggest) first, around 2550 BC; King Khafra built the second pyramid around 2520 BC; King Menkaura built the third (smallest of the three and last) in about 2490 BC.

Although there are a few passageways and chambers inside each pyramid, the structures are mostly solid stone. They were designed to be permanently sealed after the bodies of the pharaohs were placed inside. Neither the inside nor the outside of the pyramid had any public function other than to memorialize the powerful king buried inside.

As impressive as they look today, the Giza pyramids were even more striking when first built. Originally, the four faces of each pyramid were covered with a smooth layer of bright white limestone blocks that would have gleamed and glittered in the sunlight. After these casing blocks fell or were stripped off hundreds of years ago, many were hauled away and used to build mosques and houses in the city of Cairo nearby.

The pyramids at Giza have been astonishing humanity for more than 4,500 years. Successive generations of travelers, invaders, and explorers have come across them and marveled: Ancient Greeks, Arab conquerors, even Napoleon.

Even in Ancient Egyptian times, the Giza pyramids were antiques. They were more than a thousand years old at the time of King Tutankhamen. The largest pyramid at Giza is the only one of the Seven Wonders of the Ancient World that remains; to this day, it is a sight that amazes all who see it.

Discuss and Decide

If you were to write a travel brochure advertising a visit to the Giza pyramids, which facts would you highlight and why?

Source 2: Data Analysis

The Great Pyramid at Giza	
Pyramid Statistics	
Height	Originally 481 feet high, the pyramid; currently stands at 450 feet. It is higher than the Statue of Liberty, St. Peter's Basilica in Rome, or Big Ben in London.
Base	Each side is 756 feet. The construction was so accurate, there is only a 7.9-inch difference between the longest and shortest sides of the base. Almost ten football fields would fit into the base.
Accuracy	The blocks were shaped and placed so perfectly that even today it is not possible to squeeze a knife blade between them.
How Was the Great Pyramid at Giza Built?	
Skilled laborers	Some archaeologists estimate it took 4,000 skilled laborers at least 20 years.
Materials	The pyramid is comprised of approximately 2,300,000 limestone and granite blocks, each weighing an average of 2.5 tons, for a total weight of 5,750,000 tons.
Transport	Some of the stone blocks were transported by boat from quarries as far as 500 miles away.
Construction	Stones were hauled into place on sleds pulled by teams of at least 30 men, without the help of engines, pulleys, or even wheeled carts.
Simple tools	The builders had copper, bronze, wood, and stone tools—no iron or steel. The Great Pyramid was built using simple, hand-held tools such as chisels, mallets, rock pounders and polishers, and small wooden clamps.
Largest pieces of stone	The largest slabs of stone are above the King's Chamber, inside the Great Pyramid. They weigh about 50 tons each.
Ramp	Archaeologists suggest that a huge ramp was built, allowing stones to be hauled to the top. The ramp would have to be raised as the pyramid grew taller.
Notable Records	
Tallest man-made structure	The Great Pyramid was the tallest man-made structure for more than 3,800 years.
Visibility	The three pyramids at Giza are visible from space.
Alignment	The four sides of the Great Pyramid align almost exactly with true north, south, east, and west; without the magnetic compass, the builders probably used the stars to make their calculations.

Source 3: Travel Guide

✈ Visiting the

MaYaN PYRaMiDS

Where can I find the Mayan pyramids?

If you want to find a Mayan pyramid, go to Central America! The Maya were a Mesoamerican civilization that arose around 1500 BC. They built most of their pyramids between the 3rd and 9th century AD, all across eastern Mexico, Belize, Guatemala, Honduras, and El Salvador.

What do they look like?

While Mayan pyramids come in a variety of shapes and sizes, most are step pyramids;

The entrance to the pyramid is at the very top, not the bottom.

The ruins at Chichen Itza, a city in the Yucatán built by the Mayans.

the sides are not smooth but instead rise up in stages, like giant stairs. Often there are one or more actual staircases built on top of the steps, leading to a temple or sanctuary at the top.

Compared to the Egyptian pyramids at Giza, Mayan pyramids are mostly smaller, but steeper and more ornate. They were built of stone blocks held together with lime mortar. Some were covered with plaster and painted. The Maya were expert astronomers, so their pyramids were positioned and constructed to note important points in the calendar, such as the solstice and equinox.

The pyramids played an important part in the religious and community life of the people.

Looking up the terraces toward the top of the pyramid.

Mayan pyramids functioned as temples, whether or not they were also tombs of high-ranking officials. Only priests were allowed to climb the stairs to the top. There they performed religious rituals including sacrifices. The pyramids were often part of large complexes that included palaces, ball courts, plazas, and courtyards.

Sometimes a new pyramid was built on top of an old one. If you were to dig down inside a Mayan pyramid built in, say, 800 AD, you might find the ruins of one built hundreds of years earlier.

What else do I need to know for my visit?
Mayan civilization flourished between around 250 and 900 AD, at which point it went into a sudden and mysterious decline. Many cities and towns were abandoned and completely swallowed up by the jungle. Although the local people may have known about them—and although Spanish conquistadors had written about them—many of the most impressive Mayan archeological sites were not "rediscovered" by Europeans until 1839 and later. Even now there are Mayan pyramids hiding in the thick jungle, waiting to be "discovered" by an intrepid explorer.

Maybe that explorer will be you!

The Mayan Civilization

Discuss and Decide

Explain at least three differences between Mayan and Egyptian pyramids, and the reason for one of these differences. Cite text evidence in your discussion.

Source 4: Infographic

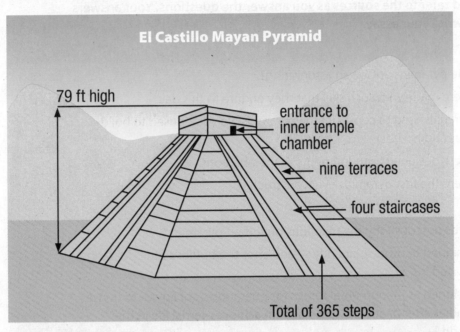

El Castillo Mayan Pyramid

79 ft high

entrance to
inner temple
chamber

nine terraces

four staircases

Total of 365 steps

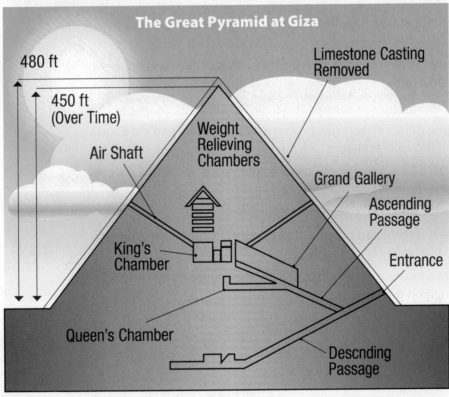

The Great Pyramid at Giza

480 ft

450 ft
(Over Time)

Limestone Casting
Removed

Air Shaft

Weight
Relieving
Chambers

Grand Gallery

Ascending
Passage

King's
Chamber

Entrance

Queen's Chamber

Descnding
Passage

Discuss and Decide

What information about Egyptian pyramids does the infographic provide that
the previous two sources do not?

Respond to Questions on Step 2 Sources

The following questions will help you think about the sources you've read. Use your notes and refer to the sources as you answer the questions. Your answers will help you write your essay.

1 Why are the pyramids at Giza so astonishing?

  a. They were made with such skill that they endure to this day.

  b. The materials used to construct the pyramids were later used to build mosques and houses.

  c. They were designed as monuments to the pharaohs.

  d. They were the first pyramids ever constructed.

2 Which words describe why the pharaohs built their pyramids?

  a. " . . . designed to be permanently sealed after the bodies of the pharaohs were placed inside."

  b. " . . . designed as monumental tombs for pharaohs . . . of Egypt, to house their bodies after death and to help them achieve eternal life in the afterworld."

  c. "The pyramids at Giza have been astonishing humanity for more than 4,500 years."

  d. " . . . many were hauled away and used to build mosques and houses in the city of Cairo nearby."

3 Which of the reasons below might explain why the entrance to the Mayan pyramids was located at the top?

  a. The Mayans did not have the skill to place entrances at the base of the pyramids.

  b. The Mayans were afraid to visit the tombs below.

  c. The Mayans constructed the pyramids to note important astronomical events.

  d. The pyramids were built on top of one another, covering up entrances that once existed on the bottom.

1. Analyze   2. Practice   3. Perform

4 Which of the following claims is *not* true?

   a. The pyramids at Giza were built by different pharaohs.

   b. The pyramids at Giza are visible from space.

   c. The staircases on Mayan pyramids played a role in religious rituals.

   d. The pyramids at Giza were less stunning when they were first built.

5 Which of the selections below best support the correct claim in Question 4?

   a. "Mayan pyramids functioned as temples, whether or not they were also tombs."

   b. "King Khufu built the Great Pyramid (the biggest) first, around 2550 BC . . ."

   c. "Even in Ancient Egyptian times the Giza pyramids were antiques."

   d. ". . . the faces of each pyramid were covered with a smooth layer of bright white limestone blocks that would have gleamed . . ."

6 **Prose Constructed-Response** What do the graphic representations of the Mayan pyramid and the Great Pyramid at Giza help you better understand about pyramids? Explain.

_____

_____

_____

_____

7 **Prose Constructed-Response** What is the main idea of the article "The Pyramids of Giza"? Be sure to state the main idea of the selection, as well as its supporting details. Cite text evidence in your response.

_____

_____

_____

_____

Planning and Prewriting

When you write a compare-and-contrast essay, first decide what main idea your reading brings to mind. For your essay, you should find facts that show similarities and differences between the two types of pyramids.

 You may prefer to do your planning on your computer.

Decide on Key Points

Summarize the key points that you will include in your essay.

Characteristics	Mayan Pyramids	Egyptian Pyramids
1. Physical Appearance		
2. Purpose		
3. Construction Method		
4. Permanence		

Developing Your Topic

Before you write your essay, decide how you want to arrange your ideas. You can use one of the patterns of organizing described below or come up with your own arrangement—whatever works best for your subject. Your essay will begin with an introductory paragraph and end with a concluding paragraph.

Point-by-Point Discuss the first point of comparison or contrast for both topics, then move on to the second point. You read across the rows of this chart.

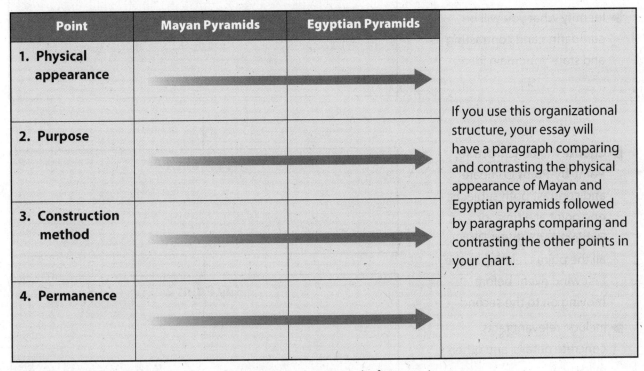

Point	Mayan Pyramids	Egyptian Pyramids	
1. Physical appearance			If you use this organizational structure, your essay will have a paragraph comparing and contrasting the physical appearance of Mayan and Egyptian pyramids followed by paragraphs comparing and contrasting the other points in your chart.
2. Purpose			
3. Construction method			
4. Permanence			

Subject-by-Subject Discuss all the points about one topic before moving on to the next. You read across the rows of this chart.

Selection	Physical Appearance	Purpose	Construction Method	Permanence
1. Mayan pyramids				
2. Egyptian pyramids				
If you use this organizational structure, your essay will have one or two paragraphs addressing all your points as they relate to Mayan pyramids, followed by one or two paragraphs addressing all your points as they relate to Egyptian pyramids.				

Finalize Your Plan

Use your responses and notes from previous pages to create a detailed plan for your essay. Fill in the chart below.

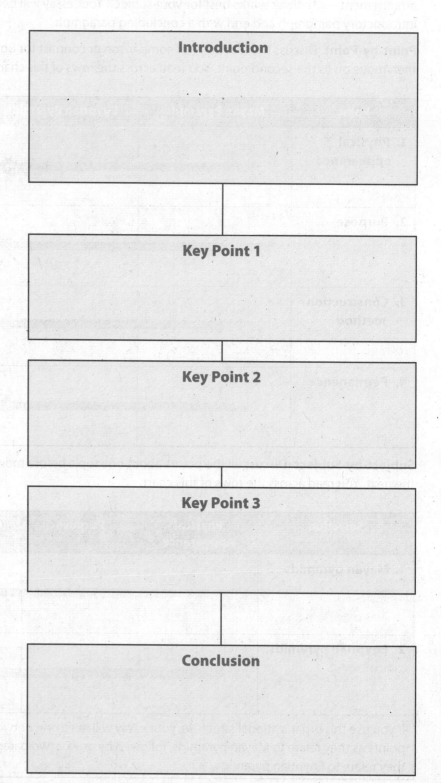

▶ Hook your audience with an interesting detail, question, or quotation.

▶ Identify what you will be comparing and contrasting and state your main idea.

Introduction

▶ Choose the text structure: **Point-by-Point** Compare and contrast both subjects, one point at a time; or **Subject-by-Subject** Discuss all the points relating to the first wind event before moving on to the second.

▶ Include relevant facts, concrete details, and other evidence.

Key Point 1

Key Point 2

Key Point 3

▶ Summarize the key points and restate your main idea.

▶ Include an insight that follows from and supports your main idea.

Conclusion

Draft Your Essay

▶ **Your Audience:** Your teacher

▶ **Your Purpose:** Demonstrate your understanding of the specific requirements of an informative essay with a comparison/contrast text structure.

▶ **Style:** Use a formal and objective tone.

▶ **Transitions:** Use words and phrases such as *for example* or *because* to create cohesion, or flow.

Revise

Revision Checklist: Self Evaluation

 If you drafted your essay on the computer, you may wish to print it out so that you can more easily evaluate it.

Use the checklist below to guide your analysis.

Ask Yourself	Tips	Revision Strategies
1. Does the introduction grab the audience's attention?	Underline sentences in the introduction that engage readers.	Add an interesting question, fact, or observation to get the reader's attention.
2. Is each point of comparison supported by textual evidence, facts, and concrete details?	Circle textual evidence.	Add textual evidence if necessary.
3. Are appropriate and varied transitions used to connect and contrast ideas?	Place a checkmark next to each transitional word or phrase.	Add transitional words or phrases where needed to clarify the relationships between ideas.
4. Does the concluding section sum up key ideas? Does it give the audience something to think about?	Double underline the summary of key points in the concluding section. Underline the insight offered to readers.	Add an overarching view of key points or a final observation about the significance of the comparison and contrast.

Revision Checklist: Peer Review

Exchange your essay with a classmate, or read it aloud to your partner. As you read and comment on your classmate's essay, focus on how clearly the comparison and contrast have been supported by details. Help each other identify parts of the drafts that need strengthening, reworking, or even a complete new approach.

What To Look For	Notes for My Partner
1. Does the introduction grab the audience's attention?	
2. Is each point of comparison supported by textual evidence, facts, and concrete details?	
3. Are appropriate and varied transitions used to connect and contrast ideas?	
4. Does the concluding section sum up key ideas? Does it give the audience something to think about?	

Edit

 Edit your essay to correct spelling, grammar, and punctuation errors.

In what ways were the Maya, the Aztecs, and the Inca advanced for their time?

You will read:

▶ **THREE INFORMATIVE ARTICLES**

Mayan Civilization

Aztecs

The Inca

You will write:

▶ **AN INFORMATIVE ESSAY**

In what ways were the Maya, the Aztecs, and the Inca advanced for their time?

Mayan Civilization
by Suzanne Hopkins

Image Credits: ©Digital Vision/Getty Images

AS YOU READ *Identify key terms that you might want to use in your essay.*

NOTES

Long before the rise of the Inca and Aztec Empires, Mayan civilization flourished in Central America. The Maya first settled in the region as early as 1500 BC, growing maize and living in small agricultural communities. But by about AD 200, these villages were becoming cities. At its height, Mayan civilization included more than 40 cities, each with a population of 5,000 to 50,000 people. The cities had huge stone buildings, including palaces, pyramids, and temples. Each city-state was ruled by a king.

Mayan Society

10 Mayan society was hierarchical, divided by both class and profession. Below the king was a class of nobles; a middle class was composed of priests and commoners; at the lowest level were slaves.

The Maya were never an empire. Although the cities shared the same culture, each operated independently. They traded goods with each other, including salt, shells, cotton, corn, rubber, incense, feathers, jade, flint, obsidian, and granite were carried in huge dugout canoes along rivers and around coasts. They also fought wars, but these were on a small scale, one city against another.

A Time of Prosperity

For many centuries, the Maya prospered. They studied the stars and developed sophisticated and accurate calendars; practiced elaborate
20 (if gory) religious rituals and worshiped a crowded pantheon of gods and goddesses; they developed complex hieroglyphic writing that they

used to record historical and religious events; they had a mathematical system based on the unit 20. Their craftsmen and artists produced fine goods made of cotton, feathers, clay, wood, and precious metals and stones, among other materials.

Decline

Yet by AD 800, Mayan civilization was in decline. While the reasons are not fully understood, archaeologists believe that the cities had grown so large, there were not enough farmers left to supply them with food. In addition, the farmland was becoming overused, the soil
30 depleted. Food production plummeted, and famine forced people to leave the urban centers.

By AD 950, the great Mayan cities were mostly abandoned, the population dispersed into small agricultural villages. The jungle swallowed up the empty cities. The Mayan people, however, were still around when the Spanish conquistadors arrived. And they are still around today.

Though the Spanish conquered the Maya in the mid-1500s and founded cities on Mayan lands, temples and monuments remain as a testimony to the Mayans' achievements. These structures attract
40 tourists from around the world, ensuring that the Maya will never be forgotten.

Close Read

1. Cite at least two reasons the Maya prospered as a civilization.

_____

_____

_____

2. Explain possible reasons for the decline of the Mayan empire. Cite text evidence in your response.

_____

_____

_____

AZTECS

by Jose Maldonado

© Houghton Mifflin Harcourt Publishing Company • Image Credits: ©Don Couch/Houghton Mifflin Harcourt

AS YOU READ *Identify details that support the main idea.*

NOTES

Long ago, around AD 1345, a group of people in central Mexico wandered in search of a new home. These people were the Aztecs, and Aztec legend says that a prophesy led them to a group of islands on Lake Texcoco, in the Valley of Mexico. Their settlement would eventually become the great city Tenochtitlán.

As the last to arrive, the Aztec were at first ruled over by more powerful city-states in the area. But, after making alliances with some of these city-states, the Aztecs were able to defeat their overlords in 1428. Soon they began conquering other tribes across Mexico, and

10 Tenochtitlán became the center of a powerful Aztec empire.

The Great City

At its height in 1519, the city covered about five square miles and had between 250 and 400 thousand inhabitants. It had temples, palaces, a great market, houses, and gardens. Although the city was built on a swamp, the Aztecs were able to adapt. They traveled around and through Tenochtitlán by canoe. Several raised causeways connected the island city to the mainland. They farmed special plots of land called chinampas (also known as "floating gardens")—raised areas of land built in the lake, separated by canals, where they grew maize and other crops.

20 Building cities was not the Aztecs' only accomplishment. They used picture writing to record political and religious history; they used calendars and had a mathematical system based on the number 20. They wove cotton cloth, made pottery, carved in stone and other materials, made musical instruments and elaborate costumes of feathers.

A Hierarchical Society

Aztec society was strictly hierarchical, ruled over by a godlike emperor. Religion was an important part of everyday life, and a gory one, as they believed that human sacrifice was needed to keep the sun alive. The Aztec were harsh rulers; they demanded high tributes and
30 were constantly fighting in order to keep up a steady supply of captives to use as human sacrifice. The harsh way they ruled their empire helped to undermine them in the end.

Decline

In 1519, Hernán Cortés and his army arrived in Tenochtitlán. When the Spanish first saw the city, they thought they must be dreaming. It was larger and more impressive than any Spanish city of the time. Vastly outnumbered, the Spanish conquistador took the Aztec emperor Montezuma II hostage and began a siege in Tenochtitlán that the Aztec could not withstand. Within three years, and with the help of the local Indian tribes who were eager to break away from Aztec rule, Cortes was
40 able to crush the Aztecs and bring about the complete collapse of their empire. The last Aztec emperor surrendered the city to Cortés in 1521, thus ending one of the most famous empires in history.

Close Read

1. Why did the Spanish think "they must be dreaming" when they saw Tenochtitlán? Cite text evidence in your response.

_____

_____

_____

2. Cite two reasons from the text showing how the Aztecs' harsh rule contributed to the fall of their society.

_____

_____

_____

_____

Source 3: Informative Article

THE INCA

by Akbar Patel

AS YOU READ *Identify topics addressed in this article that have also been addressed in the previous two.*

NOTES

Sometime in the twelfth century BC, the first Inca ruler is said to have moved his tribe to what is now Cuzco, high in the Andes. Until the fourteenth century, the Inca lived there peacefully with their neighbors. But then they began a campaign of territorial expansion that would eventually make Cuzco the capital of a vast empire.

Establishing an Empire

Successive generations of Incan rulers worked to expand Incan territory through war and conquest. At its height, the Inca Empire stretched more than 2,000 miles along the west coast of South America and governed millions of people. The farthest reaches of the empire
10 were connected with well-constructed roads and strong rope bridges. An elaborate system of relay runners enabled messages to be carried 250 miles a day; runners made the 1,250-mile journey from Quito (a city in the far north) to Cuzco in just five days.

Incan society was hierarchical and highly centralized, with the god-like emperor at the top of the social pyramid, followed by provincial governors, local rulers and leaders, and finally the common people. The common people paid taxes and tributes and worked for the central government. The Inca did not have a writing system, but they were able to keep track of trade goods and stockpiles with a special system of
20 knotted strings called a quipu. Religion was an important part of life.

1. Analyze 2. Practice 3. Perform

Economy

The Inca were farmers, growing potatoes as well as other crops, often in terraces cut into the high mountainsides. They had llamas to carry loads, for wool, and for meat. They were also skilled craftsmen, building impressive cities of stone, weaving exquisite woolen cloth, and making pottery, jewelry, and many other useful and ornamental objects.

Decline

The Spanish conquistador Francisco Pizarro arrived in Peru in 1531—a very bad time for the Inca. An emperor had died, and his two sons fought over the succession. In the ensuing war, cities were devastated, the economy was damaged, and the Inca empire was
30 divided. Pizarro used his guns, horses, and some trickery to easily defeat the Inca. New diseases brought to the Americas by the Spanish weakened the Inca as well.

Incan civilization was wiped out, but they left behind plenty of evidence of their achievements. The Incan city of Machu Picchu, for example, was never known to the Spanish invaders, but you can visit it today.

Close Read

1. What was unique about the way that the Inca were able to expand their empire? Cite text evidence in your response.

_____

_____

_____

_____

2. Cite evidence of the Incas' success as a civilization.

_____

_____

_____

_____

Respond to Questions on Step 3 Sources

Read the following questions and choose the best answer for each.

1 Which of the following claims applies only to the Aztec civilization?

  a. The Aztec were conquered by the Spanish.

  b. The Aztec were harsh rulers.

  c. The Aztec were skilled boatsmen.

  d. The Aztec were part of an empire.

2 Which text below provides the best evidence to support the claim in Question 1?

  a. "They traveled around and through Tenochtitlán by canoe."

  b. "The last Aztec emperor surrendered the city to Cortés in 1521, thus ending one of the most famous empires in history."

  c. "The Maya were never an empire. Although the cities shared the same culture . . ."

  d. "Incan society was hierarchical and highly centralized, with the godlike emperor at the top . . ."

3 **Prose Constructed-Response** What factors contributed to the decline of each empire? Cite evidence from the selections in your response.

_____

_____

_____

_____

4 **Prose Constructed-Response** How was each society organized? Use details from the selections in your response.

_____

_____

_____

_____

Part 2: Write

Plan

Use the graphic organizer to help you outline the structure of your informational essay.

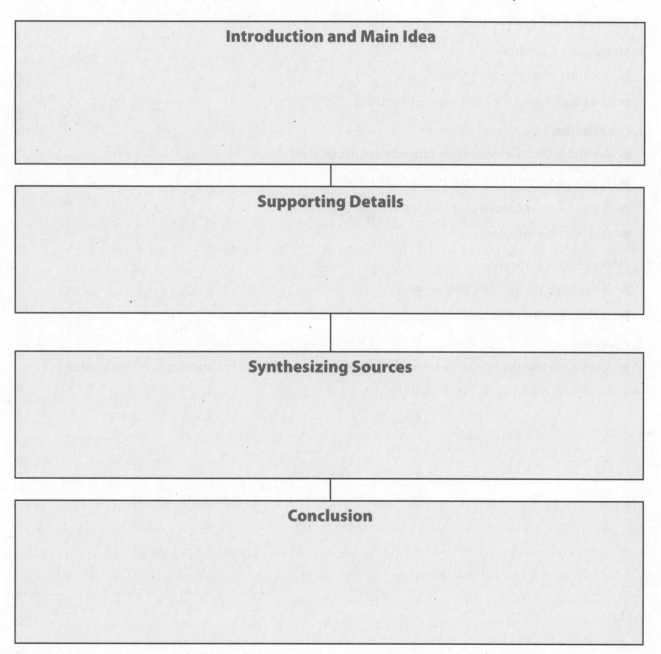

Introduction and Main Idea

Supporting Details

Synthesizing Sources

Conclusion

Draft

 Use your notes and completed graphic organizer to write a first draft of your essay.

Revise and Edit

 Look back over your essay and compare it to the Evaluation Criteria. Revise your essay and edit it to correct spelling, grammar, and punctuation errors.

Evaluation Criteria

Your teacher will be looking for:

1. *Statement of purpose*

▶ Is it clear what the main idea is?

▶ Did you support the main idea with details?

2. *Organization*

▶ Are the sections of your essay organized in a logical way?

▶ Is there a smooth flow from beginning to end?

▶ Is there a clear conclusion that supports the main idea?

▶ Did you stay on topic?

3. *Elaboration of evidence*

▶ Is the evidence relevant to the topic?

▶ Is there enough evidence?

4. *Conventions*

▶ Did you follow the rules of grammar usage as well as punctuation, capitalization, and spelling?

Changes

Literary Analysis

STEP 1
ANALYZE THE MODEL

Evaluate an analysis of E. E. Cummings's poem "Spring is like a perhaps hand."

STEP 2
PRACTICE THE TASK

Write an analysis of how Shakespeare uses irony in Mark Antony's speech.

STEP 3
PERFORM THE TASK

Write a literary analysis about the ways in which Elizabeth Barrett Browning's life experiences influenced her poetry.

Unlike nonfiction texts, literary texts—poems, stories, dramas—are not written solely to give information. They are written primarily to have an effect on the reader.

At its best, literature can cause you to react on many levels. You can be gripped by a story line or charmed by a character. The words might create a beautiful image in your mind. The mood may capture your imagination and even alter your own mood as you read.

Good literature can change readers, whether it is for the time they are reading or for a long time afterward. For example, the 19th century American philosopher and writer Henry David Thoreau championed civil disobedience as a form of protest and was inspired by the poems of Percy Bysshe Shelley. Shelley was an English Romantic poet and activist writing many decades earlier.

IN THIS UNIT, you will analyze another student's response to a free verse poem by E. E. Cummings. Then you will write an analysis of the use of irony in Mark Antony's speech in Shakespeare's *Julius Caesar*. Finally, you will read a sonnet by Elizabeth Barrett Browning written for Robert Browning, as well as the first two letters they wrote to each other that sparked their historic romance.

How does the coming of spring change us?

You will read:

▶ **A BIOGRAPHY**
E.E. Cummings: The Poet and His Craft

▶ **A POEM**
"Spring is like a perhaps hand"

You will analyze:

▶ **A STUDENT MODEL**
Winter Becomes Spring

Source Materials for Step 1

Mr. Winter assigned his class a poem by E.E. Cummings to read and analyze. He provided the following biography of the poet as well. The notes in the side column were written by Valerie Jones, a student in Mr. Winter's class.

E.E. Cummings: The Poet and His Craft

E.E. Cummings (1894–1962) started writing poetry when he was eight years old and continued writing a poem every day until age twenty-two, when he received a degree from Harvard University. After he read some ancient classical poetry, suddenly, as he put it, "an unknown and unknowable bird started singing."

I'll assume he's a smart guy!

During World War I, Cummings was an ambulance driver in France. He was mistakenly arrested for treason and clapped into detention for three months. The experience was a turning point in his life. In prison, Cummings discovered his passion for freedom and personal growth. Over the next four decades he celebrated these passions.

The following quotation is from the preface to a book of Cummings's poems. The words appear here just as he wrote them.

"The poems to come are for you and for me and are not for mostpeople
—it's no use trying to pretend that mostpeople and ourselves are alike. Mostpeople have less in common with ourselves than the squarerootofminusone. You and I are human beings;mostpeople are snobs. . . ."

Hmm . . . Why are the words bumping into each other?

In his writing, Cummings liked to use lowercase letters, unusual word spacing (words often bump together), and his own brand of punctuation. Even though his style is new, his themes are familiar. Cummings, like lyric poets throughout the ages, celebrates the joy and wonder of life and the glory of the individual.

AHA! Cummings likes breaking rules. I may love his poetry!

Discuss and Decide

With a group, discuss whether you agree with Cummings's assertion "You and I are human beings;most people are snobs." Cite text evidence in your discussion.

1. Analyze   2. Practice   3. Perform

Spring is like a perhaps hand

by E.E. Cummings

a "perhaps" hand—huh?

Spring is like a perhaps hand

(which comes carefully

out of Nowhere) arranging

a window, into which people look (while

people stare

people looking into a window and staring out?

arranging and changing placing

carefully there a strange

thing and a known thing here) and

changing everything carefully

a simile

spring is like a perhaps

"Hand" now spelled with a capital letter.

Hand in a window

(carefully to

and fro moving New and

Old things, while

people stare carefully

moving a perhaps

parenthesis?

fraction of flower here placing

an inch of air there) and

Only 5 capital letters? Why?

without breaking anything.

Discuss and Decide

Review Valerie's notes in the side column. Then discuss your initial reactions to the poem with a partner. How are your reactions like or unlike Valerie's? Cite specific evidence from the text.

Analyze a Student Model for Step 1

Read Valerie's literary analysis closely. The red side notes are the comments from her teacher, Mr. Winter.

Valerie Jones
Mr. Winter, English
March 24

Winter Becomes Spring

Good that you used these terms.

In the lyric poem "Spring is like a perhaps hand," E.E. Cummings uses a simile to compare spring to a hand rearranging items in a window display. His free verse poem is full of unusual word choices and odd capitalization and punctuation. He creates an image of the gradual and uncertain morphing of winter into spring.

Important concept! Bringing it in early is helpful to the reader.

My experience of spring, here in the rural Northeast, is that it can be hard to know exactly when winter becomes spring. We can often see the old remnants of winter, with new spring elements peeking through. There might still be snow on the ground near where the first green shoots of daffodils are pushing up through the bare earth. Maybe spring has come, or maybe—perhaps—the wintery weather will continue.

Your observations on the transition to spring are useful.

E.E. Cummings writes about the same seasonal change in this poem. His setting seems to be a town. He describes a home or a shop with a window display and shows a hand arranging old and new items in it while passers-by stop to watch. He says that spring is like this hand. The new items in spring are things like flowers and air.

It's interesting that Cummings capitalizes only five words, *Spring, Hand, Nowhere, Old,* and *New.* These words are probably the most important ones in the poem. Spring is the topic. The words *Old* and *New* stress the change from old winter to new spring. The *Hand* is the poem's key image. *Perhaps* may be meant to caution readers that spring may not really have arrived.

Why does Cummings place *perhaps* in such an odd position in the sentence "Spring is like a perhaps hand"? The word forced me to slow down and concentrate more closely. It made me wonder whose hand was being described and why it was changing everything carefully. Maybe Cummings was saying that we can't always be certain that spring has arrived. To me, the resolution of the poem comes in the final line, "without breaking anything." Spring might come slowly, but it does come at last.

The capitals are odd, but your explanation is interesting and plausible.

I really like your guess about "perhaps"! And perhaps you are right, Valerie! Very good job!

Discuss and Decide

With a group, decide whether or not you agree with Valerie's interpretation of the poem. Cite text evidence in your response.

© Houghton Mifflin Harcourt Publishing Company

Terminology of Literary Analysis

Read each term and explanation. Then look back at Valerie Jones's literary analysis and find an example to complete the chart.

Term	Explanation	Example from Valerie's Essay
controlling idea	The **controlling idea** is the main observation or assertion about the poem or literary work.	
theme	The **theme** is the underlying message about life or human nature that the writer wants the reader to understand.	
tone	The **tone** is the attitude the writer takes toward a subject.	
figurative language	**Figurative language** is language that communicates meanings beyond the literal meanings of words. Similes, metaphors, and personification are examples of figurative language.	
style	The **style** is the particular way in which a work of literature is written—not *what* is said but *how* it is said.	
voice	The **voice** is a writer's unique use of language that allows a reader to "hear" a human personality in the writer's work.	

*How can the use of irony
change our ideas?*

You will read:

▶ **A BIOGRAPHY**
  Mark Antony

▶ **A HISTORICAL NOTE**
  *Caesar's Death and Shakespeare's
  Play*

▶ **AN INFORMATIONAL TEXT**
  Irony in Literature

▶ **A SPEECH**
  *Mark Antony's speech
  from* The Tragedy of Julius Caesar,
  Act III. Scene 2.

You will write:

▶ **A LITERARY ANALYSIS**
  *How does Shakespeare use irony in
  Mark Antony's speech?*

Source Materials for Step 2

AS YOU READ You will be writing an essay analyzing the use of irony in a famous Shakespearean speech. Carefully study the sources in Step 2. As you read, underline and circle information that may be useful to you when you write your essay.

SOURCE 1: Biography

MARK ANTONY

Along with Julius Caesar, Mark Antony was one of the best-known and most powerful men in Rome in the first century BC. Born in 83 BC to a family that today would be considered middle class, Antony followed in the footsteps of his father, a military commander, and gained his own fame as a cavalry officer after winning important battles for the Roman army.

In 54 BC, Antony was sent to Gaul (the ancient name for France) as an officer for Julius Caesar. The two men forged a friendship that lasted until Caesar's death. As Caesar rose to political power, he saw to it that Antony was chosen for several
10 important positions. In the Republican Civil War, Antony served as Caesar's second in command and together they defeated other powerful Roman leaders. In 44 BC, Caesar and Antony became co-consuls of Rome, the highest elected officials of the Republic.

One year earlier, the Roman Senate had declared Caesar dictator for life. However, some in the Senate feared that he would become a tyrant and began plotting to have Caesar killed. When rumors of a conspiracy against Caesar started circulating, Mark Antony rushed to alert his friend but was unable to reach him. On March 15, 44 BC, Caesar was assassinated. After his funeral oration for Caesar, Antony feared for his own life, so he fled Rome disguised as a slave. However, he soon returned to take charge of Caesar's will. When the will was made public, it revealed that Caesar had left
20 his gardens to the people of Rome and a sum of money to every Roman living in the city. Caesar's will turned the people of Rome against the assassins, since it seemed to prove that Caesar had loved his country.

Discuss and Decide

Think about Mark Antony's relationship with Caesar. What goal might he have had in mind by giving his speech at Caesar's funeral? Cite text evidence in your discussion.

| 1. Analyze | 2. Practice | 3. Perform |

© Houghton Mifflin Harcourt Publishing Company • Image Credits: ©Fernando Cortes/Shutterstock

Caesar's Death and Shakespeare's Play

Shakespeare's play *Julius Caesar* is based on the historical events of 44 BC surrounding the death of Julius Caesar. Caesar, dictator of Rome, had made many enemies during his ascent to power. He was assassinated on March 15 by a group of senators including Brutus, a one-time supporter and friend of Caesar who nonetheless was convinced that the dictator's arrogance and power needed to be stopped.

In the play, Caesar's close friend Mark Antony, in danger himself from the assassins, wants to shift public opinion of Caesar by speaking at his funeral. Antony convinces Brutus that the assassins have nothing to fear from him,
10   so Brutus grants him permission to speak, with four conditions:

- ■ Brutus would speak first.
- ■ Mark Antony would speak immediately afterwards.
- ■ Antony would not blame the conspirators.
- ■ Antony would admit that he spoke with the conspirators' permission.

Brutus does speak first to the people of Rome and explains why he took part in the killing of Caesar: "Not that I loved Caesar less, but that I loved Rome more." Brutus presents himself as "an honourable man" and Caesar as an ambitious leader who would have enslaved the Romans. Then Antony enters with Caesar's body, and begins to speak, using Brutus's own words to sway
20   public opinion against the conspirators.

Discuss and Decide

Think about what the assassins have done. Why might Mark Antony believe his life is in danger? Cite text evidence in your discussion.

What Is . . .

Irony in Literature

by Erica Duvall

Irony is a discrepancy or contradiction between what is said and what is meant, or between what happens and what is expected to happen. There are three main kinds of irony in literature.

Situational irony: A team wins the crucial basketball game only to see its leading player injured in a car accident. Someone qualifies for a competition just before the competition is canceled for lack of funds. A character tries to avoid a threat by changing his or her actions and encounters another threat instead. A person who rarely does well ends up experiencing a sudden triumph over adversity. These famous lines from Coleridge's poem, "The Rime of the Ancient Mariner" contain a great

10 example: "Water, water, every where, / Nor any drop to drink." Because situational irony is unexpected, it generally serves to shock readers rather than to create the tension of anticipation.

Dramatic (or tragic) **irony:** A character's words or actions convey something that is understood by readers (or the audience in the case of a play) but not by the character. This may be because the audience or readers are aware of an earlier event that the character has not witnessed or heard about. An author or playwright might use dramatic irony to increase tension, allowing the readers or audience to foresee danger that the character cannot anticipate. In *The Tragedy of Romeo and Juliet*, the audience knows Juliet drank a sleeping potion, but Romeo thinks she's dead, leading to his own

20 demise. The tension within the play builds with this realization.

Verbal irony: Someone says something that means one thing but is intended to mean the opposite. Sometimes a character uses irony to deliver a veiled insult while seeming to praise the person being insulted. In *The Tragedy of Julius Caesar*, each time Mark Antony repeats, "Brutus is an honourable man," we begin to wonder if, in fact, he is. Irony may be humorous or bitter, and it may or may not be obvious to its intended target. A character may use irony from a number of motives, including malice, anger, or merely the desire to be witty.

Source 4: Speech

from **The Tragedy of Julius Caesar**, Act III. Scene 2. *by* **William Shakespeare**

After Brutus speaks to the Roman people, Mark Antony enters with Caesar's body and begins to speak.

NOTES

Friends, Romans, countrymen, lend me your ears;
I come to bury Caesar, not to praise him.
The evil that men do lives after them;
The good is oft interred with their bones;
5   So let it be with Caesar. The noble Brutus
Hath told you Caesar was ambitious:
If it were so, it was a grievous fault,
And grievously hath Caesar answer'd it.
Here, under leave of Brutus and the rest,—
10   For Brutus is an honourable man;
So are they all, all honourable men—
Come I to speak in Caesar's funeral.
He was my friend, faithful and just to me:
But Brutus says he was ambitious;
15   And Brutus is an honourable man.
He hath brought many captives home to Rome,
Whose ransoms did the general coffers fill:
Did this in Caesar seem ambitious?
When that the poor have cried, Caesar hath wept:
20   Ambition should be made of sterner stuff:
Yet Brutus says he was ambitious;
And Brutus is an honourable man.
You all did see that on the Lupercal°
I thrice presented him a kingly crown,
25   Which he did thrice refuse: was this ambition?
Yet Brutus says he was ambitious;
And, sure, he is an honourable man.
I speak not to disprove what Brutus spoke,
But here I am to speak what I do know.
30   You all did love him once, not without cause:
What cause withholds you then, to mourn for him?
O judgment! thou art fled to brutish beasts,
And men have lost their reason. Bear with me;
My heart is in the coffin there with Caesar,
35   And I must pause till it come back to me.

---

23. Lupercal: a festival honoring Pan

Discuss and Decide

Does Antony follow through with his opening statement? Cite text evidence.

Respond to Questions on Step 2 Sources

These questions will help you analyze the sources you've read. Use your notes and refer back to the sources in order to answer the questions. Your answers will help you write your essay.

1 Why does Antony use Caesar's will to persuade the people that Caesar was not a tyrant?

   a. He wants the crowd to murder the conspirators.

   b. He wants the people to realize that Brutus wants to gain power.

   c. He wants the crowd to know that Brutus was jealous of Caesar.

   d. He wants the people of Rome to turn against the conspirators.

2 Antony says "Brutus is an "honourable" man." Why does he repeatedly use this phrase? Antony wants to—

   a. convince the crowd that Brutus murdered Caesar.

   b. show that Brutus is actually dishonorable.

   c. prove that he is a better leader than Brutus.

   d. explain to the crowd why Brutus is admirable.

3 Which best summarizes what Antony is trying to do in his speech? Antony is trying to—

   a. get Brutus and the other conspirators to admit they are murderers.

   b. teach the crowd about Caesar's life.

   c. make the crowd see that Caesar was not a tyrant.

   d. protect Brutus and the other conspirators.

4 Select the three pieces of evidence from Mark Antony's speech that best support your answer to Question 1.

   a. "Friends, Romans, countrymen, lend me your ears" (line 1)

   b. "...The noble Brutus / Hath told you Caesar was ambitious" (lines 5–6)

   c. "Here, under leave of Brutus and the rest,—" (line 9)

   d. "When that the poor have cried, Caesar hath wept" (line 19)

   e. "I thrice presented him a kingly crown, / Which he did thrice refuse: was this ambition?" (lines 24–25)

   f. "I speak not to disprove what Brutus spoke" (line 28)

   g. "But here I am to speak what I do know." (line 29)

   h. "You all did love him once, not without cause" (line 30)

5 **Prose Constructed-Response** In what way was Mark Antony a loyal friend to Caesar? Cite evidence from his biography in your answer.

_____

_____

_____

_____

6 **Prose Constructed-Response** Why do you think Brutus put so many conditions on Antony's speech? What do you think Brutus is afraid of? Cite evidence from Source 2.

_____

_____

_____

_____

_____

7 **Prose Constructed-Response** Given the circumstances that surround the speech, why is irony a key tool for Antony to be able to safely achieve his goal? What kind of irony does he use?

_____

_____

_____

_____

_____

Write a literary analysis that answers the question:
How does Shakespeare use irony in Mark Antony's
speech?

Planning and Prewriting

Analyze the Sources

You have read a variety of texts that helped you understand the context of Mark
Antony's speech. Think about how this information helped you understand Mark
Antony's intentions. In the chart below, cite a fact or detail from each source that
adds to the irony in his speech.

Source	Fact or detail	How does this add to the irony of his speech?
Biography Mark Antony		
Historical Note Caesar's Death and Shakespeare's Play		
Informational Text Irony in Literature		

1. Analyze   2. Practice   3. Perform

Write Your Main Idea

Review your notes. In his speech, Mark Antony uses irony to express his most important ideas. Explain the use of irony in the lines below. Then state the main idea of the speech.

" . . . The noble Brutus
Hath told you Caesar was ambitious:
If it were so, it was a grievous fault,
And grievously hath Caesar answer'd it.
Here, under leave of Brutus and the rest,—
 For Brutus is an honourable man;
So are they all, all honourable men—" (lines 5–11)

_____

_____

"But Brutus says he was ambitious;
And Brutus is an honourable man.
He hath brought many captives home to Rome,
Whose ransoms did the general coffers fill:
Did this in Caesar seem ambitious?
When that the poor have cried, Caesar hath wept:
Ambition should be made of sterner stuff:
Yet Brutus says he was ambitious;
And Brutus is an honourable man." (lines 14–22)

_____

_____

"I thrice presented him a kingly crown,
Which he did thrice refuse: was this ambition?
Yet Brutus says he was ambitious;
And, sure, he is an honourable man." (lines 24–27)

_____

_____

Main Idea

Finalize Your Plan

Organize your key points in an order that makes sense for the analysis. You can address them in order of importance or in the order in which they appear.

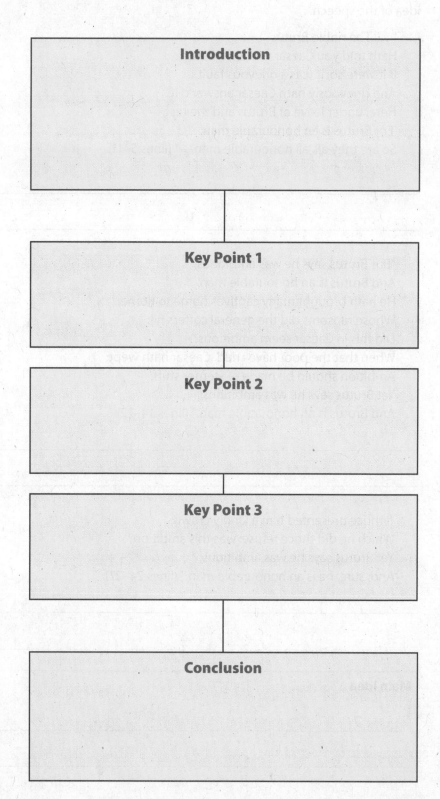

- ▶ Begin with a captivating comment, observation, or question about the reading.
- ▶ Provide necessary or interesting background information.
- ▶ Include your main idea.

Introduction

- ▶ State your first key point with support and elaboration.
- ▶ Develop a separate paragraph for each of your key points, using effective transitions between each one.
- ▶ Elaborate by explaining how each detail connects to each key point.

Key Point 1

Key Point 2

Key Point 3

- ▶ Restate your main idea using different words.
- ▶ Leave your readers with an intriguing thought.

Conclusion

Draft Your Essay

As you write, think about:

▶ **Audience:** Your teacher

▶ **Purpose:** Demonstrate your understanding of the specific requirements of a literary analysis.

▶ **Style:** Use a formal and objective tone.

▶ **Transitions:** Use words or phrases, such as *furthermore* or *in addition* to create cohesion, or flow.

Revise

Revision Checklist: Self Evaluation

Use the checklist below to guide your analysis.

 If you drafted your essay on the computer, you may wish to print it out so that you can more easily evaluate it.

Ask Yourself	Tips	Revision Strategies
1. Does the introduction capture the audience's attention?	Underline the opening question or comment.	Add a question, observation, quote, or background information.
2. Is the controlling idea clearly stated?	Put parentheses around the controlling idea.	Rewrite your controlling idea so that it is clearly stated.
3. Are points presented in order of importance with clear and varied transitions between related ideas?	Label each paragraph with a plus, check, or minus to rate the importance of its point. Circle the transitions that link the points.	Rearrange body paragraphs to present points in order of importance. Add varied transitions to connect ideas as needed.
4. Is each point illustrated with relevant textual evidence?	Place a star next to each quotation or detail from the text.	Have at least one piece of supporting evidence for each idea.
5. Is there elaboration for each supporting detail?	Put an A next to each key point, a B next to text-evidence details, and a C next to elaboration.	Add more sentences that quote, summarize, or paraphrase.
6. Does the concluding section summarize the writer's ideas and provide an insight into the author's use of irony?	Place a check mark above the restatement of the writer's ideas and circle the concluding insight.	Add a summary of main points. Include an insight on the author's use of irony.

Revision Checklist: Peer Review

Exchange your essay with a classmate, or read it aloud to your partner. As you read and comment on your classmate's essay, focus on logic, organization, and evidence—not on whether you agree with the author's claim. Help each other identify parts of the drafts that need strengthening, reworking, or a new approach.

What To Look For	Notes for My Partner
1. Does the introduction capture the audience's attention?	
2. Is the controlling idea clearly stated?	
3. Are points presented in order of importance with clear and varied transitions between related ideas?	
4. Is each point illustrated with relevant textual evidence?	
5. Is there elaboration for each supporting detail?	
6. Does the concluding section summarize the writer's ideas and provide an insight into the effect of the author's use of irony?	

Edit

 Edit your essay to correct spelling, grammar, and punctuation errors.

How do our life experiences change us?

You will read:

▶ **A BIOGRAPHY**
The Life of Elizabeth Barrett Browning

▶ **A HISTORICAL ESSAY**
The Browning Letters

▶ **A POEM**
"Sonnet 43"

▶ **TWO LETTERS**
The Letters of Robert Browning and Elizabeth Barrett Barrett

You will write:

▶ **A LITERARY ANALYSIS**
How did Elizabeth Barrett Browning's life experiences influence her poetry?

Part 1: Read Sources

Source 1: Biography

The Life of
Elizabeth Barrett Browning

by Alicia Kim

Born in 1806 in Durham, England, Elizabeth Barrett Browning was an English poet who gained enormous fame during her lifetime. The oldest of twelve children, she was born into great wealth, her father having made most of his fortune from sugar plantations that he owned in Jamaica. By all accounts, Elizabeth lived a privileged childhood, riding her pony around the grounds of her family's estate and visiting the local neighbors. Educated at home, she was something of a child prodigy. She writes that at age six she was reading novels. At age ten she was studying Greek, writing
10 her own epic poem in the Greek style two years later.

While living with her father in London, Elizabeth published her first book of mature poetry which gained her some fame. During these years in London, however, her ill-health (the exact cause of which is unknown) worsened, forcing her to spend a year on the coast with her favorite brother, Edward, who tragically drowned a year later. Distraught over her brother's death, Elizabeth returned home, becoming an invalid and a recluse, spending the next five years in her bedroom and seeing few people in her father's home on Wimpole Street.

20 Elizabeth continued to write, and in 1844 published a volume of poetry with the simple title of *Poems*. This book made her one of the most popular writers in England, and it gained the attention of the renowned poet Robert Browning, whose work she had praised in one of her poems. After reading these poems, Browning wrote to her saying, "I LOVE your verses with all my heart, dear Miss Barrett," and so begins one of the greatest love stories in literary history.

As their correspondence continued, the couple exchanged nearly 600 letters, falling in love and marrying secretly on September 12, 1846. Although most of her family accepted the marriage, Elizabeth's

30 tyrannical father disowned her, refusing to open her letters or see her.

Out of the romantic courtship between Elizabeth Barrett and Robert Browning came an outpouring of love, which Elizabeth transformed into poetry. Giving a small packet of these sonnets to Robert, which she had written to him in secret before their marriage, her husband decided to publish them, saying that he could not keep these poems to himself, for they were "the finest sonnets written in the English language since Shakespeare's." In 1850 the poems appeared as *Sonnets from the Portuguese* and included Elizabeth's

40 most famous love poem to Robert, *Sonnet 43*, beginning, "How do I love thee? Let me count the ways."

Moving to Italy after their marriage, the Brownings and their son spent many happy years there, until Elizabeth passed away, dying in Robert's arms on June 29, 1861. Of their profound love and poetry, their friend and literary critic Frederic Kenyon wrote: ". . . no modern English poet has written of love with such genius, such beauty, and such sincerity, as the two who gave the most beautiful example of it in their own lives."

NOTES

Discuss and Decide

With a small group, discuss how Elizabeth Barrett Browning's life and experiences provide a context for her work. Cite text evidence in your discussion.

Source 2: Historical Essay

The Browning Letters

by Gregory Evans

NOTES

No story of the great Victorian poets Elizabeth Barrett Browning (1806–1861) and Robert Browning (1812–1889) could be told without providing a close reading of their love letters to each other, 574 letters in all, written between January 10, 1845, and September 18, 1846. Beginning with a letter addressed to "dear Miss Barrett" and ending with Elizabeth's note to Robert as they arranged to leave England and travel to Italy a week after their marriage, the love letters of Robert and Elizabeth Barrett Browning are among the most famous in literary history, providing meaningful insights into their lives,

10 love, thoughts, feelings, experiences, and poetry.

After reading her poems for the first time, Robert Browning begins the correspondence with the line: "I LOVE your verses with all my heart, dear Miss Barrett," describing the poems as "fresh strange music," and transferring his love for her poetry into love for her before the end of the letter: "I do, as I say, love these books with all my heart—and I love you too." With that first meeting of their hearts and minds, a love affair blossoms between them. As their correspondence deepens over the course of twenty months, Elizabeth tells an acquaintance that they "are growing to be the truest of

20 friends." Yet by January 10, 1846, exactly one year after Robert's first letter, the friendship that Elizabeth has felt for him has clearly turned to love.

Elizabeth writes:

> Do you know, when you have told me to think of you, I
> have been feeling ashamed of thinking of you so much,
> of thinking of only you—which is too much
> perhaps. . . . Shall I tell you? It seems to me, to myself,
> that no man was ever before to any woman what you
> are to me. . . .

30   The rest, as they say, is history, as the most romantic literary
couple of the Victorian era falls in love through their letters and
secretly marries on September 12, 1846.

Of course, the Browning letters are only one of the series of love
letters that have survived the centuries. Love letters written by Henry
VIII to Anne Boleyn, by the poet John Keats to his beloved Fanny
Brawne, by Abigail Adams to her husband John Adams are other
notable examples. Despite the different people writing them, all these
love letters have the same purpose—to sweep the recipient of the
letter off his or her feet by a frank, even poetic, display of feelings.

40   Yet the fact that the Browning letters were written by two literary
giants attests to the letters' uniqueness. Perhaps only poets can
write of love in this way, using metaphors and symbols, making the
Browning letters unparalleled for their beauty, sincerity, and deeply
poetic display of emotion.

Close Read

Summarize the article you have just read. How did Elizabeth Barrett and
Robert Browning fall in love? Cite text evidence in your response.

_____

_____

_____

_____

_____

Sonnet 43

by Elizabeth Barrett Browning

AS YOU READ *Focus on the form of this sonnet, a 14-line poem with a definite rhyme scheme and meter. Record comments or questions about the text in the side margin.*

NOTES

How do I love thee? Let me count the ways.

I love thee to the depth and breadth and height

My soul can reach, when feeling out of sight

For the ends of Being and ideal Grace.

5   I love thee to the level of everyday's

Most quiet need, by sun and candlelight.

I love thee freely, as men strive for Right;

I love thee purely, as they turn from Praise.

I love thee with passion put to use

10   In my old griefs, and with my childhood's faith.

I love thee with a love I seemed to lose

With my lost saints,—I love thee with the breath,

Smiles, tears, of all my life!—and, if God choose,

I shall but love thee better after death.

Close Read

Reread the last six lines of the poem. How is the poet comparing the intensity of love she feels for Robert Browning with the intensity of love she had experienced earlier in her life? Cite text evidence in your response.

_____

_____

   1. Analyze   2. Practice   3. Perform

THE LETTERS OF
Robert Browning AND
Elizabeth Barrett Barrett

R.B. to E.B.B.

New Cross, Hatcham, Surrey.
[Post-mark, January 10, 1845.]

I LOVE your verses with all my heart, dear Miss Barrett,—and this is no off-hand complimentary letter that I shall write,— whatever else, no prompt matter-of-course recognition of your genius, and there a graceful and natural end of the thing. Since the day last week when I first read your poems, I quite laugh to remember how I have been turning and turning again in my mind what I should be able to tell you of their effect upon me, for in the first flush of delight I thought I would this once get out of my habit of purely passive enjoyment, when I do really enjoy, and thoroughly

10 justify my admiration—perhaps even, as a loyal fellow-craftsman should, try and find fault and do you some little good to be proud of hereafter!—but nothing comes of it all—so into me has it gone, and part of me has it become, this great living poetry of yours, not a flower of which but took root and grew. Oh, how different that is from lying to be dried and pressed flat, and prized highly, and put in a book with a proper account at top and bottom, and shut up and put away . . . and the book called a 'Flora,' besides! After all, I need not give up the thought of doing that, too, in time; because even now, talking with whoever is worthy, I can give a reason for my faith

20 in one and another excellence, the fresh strange music, the affluent language, the exquisite pathos and true new brave thought; but in this addressing myself to you—your own self, and for the first time, my feeling rises altogether. I do, as I say, love these books with all my heart—and I love you too. Do you know I was once not very far

from seeing—really seeing you? Mr. Kenyon said to me one morning 'Would you like to see Miss Barrett?' then he went to announce me,—then he returned . . . you were too unwell, and now it is years ago, and I feel as at some untoward passage in my travels, as if I had been close, so close, to some world's-wonder in chapel or crypt, only

30 a screen to push and I might have entered, but there was some slight, so it now seems, slight and just sufficient bar to admission, and the half-opened door shut, and I went home my thousands of miles, and the sight was never to be?

Well, these Poems were to be, and this true thankful joy and pride with which I feel myself,

Yours ever faithfully,
ROBERT BROWNING.

E.B.B. to R.B.

50 Wimpole Street: Jan. 11, 1845.

I thank you, dear Mr. Browning, from the bottom of my heart. You meant to give me pleasure by your letter—and even if the object had not been answered, I ought still to thank you. But it is thoroughly answered. Such a letter from such a hand! Sympathy is dear—very dear to me: but the sympathy of a poet, and of such a poet, is the quintessence of sympathy to me! Will you take back my gratitude for it?—agreeing, too, that of all the commerce done in the world, from Tyre to Carthage, the exchange of sympathy for gratitude is the most princely thing! . . .

10   Is it indeed true that I was so near to the pleasure and honour of making your acquaintance? and can it be true that you look back upon the lost opportunity with any regret? *But*—you know—if you had entered the 'crypt,' you might have caught cold, or been tired to death, and *wished* yourself 'a thousand miles off;' which would have been worse than travelling them. It is not my interest, however,

to put such thoughts in your head about its being 'all for the best';
and I would rather hope (as I do) that what I lost by one chance I
may recover by some future one. Winters shut me up as they do
dormouse's eyes; in the spring, *we shall see*: and I am so much better
20 that I seem turning round to the outward world again. And in the
meantime I have learnt to know your voice, not merely from the
poetry but from the kindness in it. Mr. Kenyon often speaks of you—
dear Mr. Kenyon!—who most unspeakably, or only speakably with
tears in my eyes,—has been my friend and helper, and my book's
friend and helper! critic and sympathiser, true friend of all hours!
You know him well enough, I think, to understand that I must be
grateful to him.

I am writing too much,—and notwithstanding that I am writing
too much, I will write of one thing more. I will say that I am your
30 debtor, not only for this cordial letter and for all the pleasure which
came with it, but in other ways, and those the highest: and I will say
that while I live to follow this divine art of poetry, in proportion to
my love for it and my devotion to it, I must be a devout admirer and
student of your works. This is in my heart to say to you—and I say it.

And, for the rest, I am proud to remain

Your obliged and faithful
ELIZABETH B. BARRETT.

Discuss and Decide

With a small group, discuss the content and tone of each letter. In what ways
are they similar? Cite text evidence in your discussion.

Respond to Questions on Step 3 Sources

These questions will help you think about the essays, the poem, and the letters you have read. Use your notes and refer to the sources in order to answer the questions. Your answers will help you write your essay.

1 **Prose Constructed-Response** What comparisons about the poet's love for Robert Browning and her religious and political beliefs does she make in the first eight lines of the sonnet? Cite specific evidence from the text.

_____

_____

_____

_____

2 **Prose Constructed-Response** What comparisons does the poet make in the last six lines of the poem?

_____

_____

_____

_____

3 **Prose Constructed-Response** How does the essay about the Browning letters help you place the two letters you have read in both a historical and a personal context?

_____

_____

_____

_____

Part 2: Write

ASSIGNMENT

Write a literary analysis that answers the question: How did Elizabeth Barrett Browning's life experiences influence her poetry, particularly "Sonnet 43," her sonnet written for Robert Browning? Support your controlling idea with evidence from the texts.

Plan

Use the graphic organizer to help you outline the structure of your literary analysis.

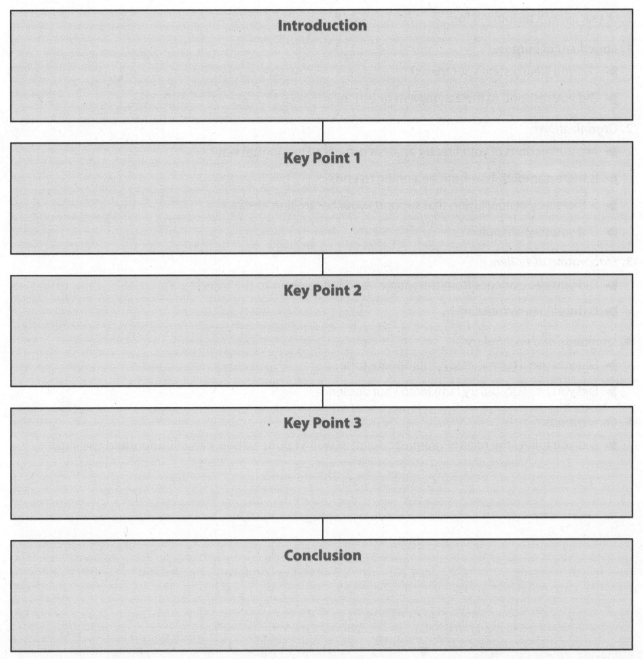

Introduction

Key Point 1

Key Point 2

Key Point 3

Conclusion

Draft

 Use your notes and completed graphic organizer to write a first draft of your literary analysis.

Revise and Edit

 Look back over your essay and compare it to the Evaluation Criteria. Revise your literary analysis and edit it to correct spelling, grammar, and punctuation errors.

Evaluation Criteria

Your teacher will be looking for:

1. *Statement of purpose*

▶ Did you clearly state your thesis?

▶ Did you respond to the assignment question?

2. *Organization*

▶ Are the sections of your literary analysis organized in a logical way?

▶ Is there a smooth flow from beginning to end?

▶ Is there a clear conclusion that supports your controlling idea?

▶ Did you stay on topic?

3. *Elaboration of evidence*

▶ Did you cite evidence from the sources, and is it relevant to the topic?

▶ Is the evidence sufficient?

4. *Language and vocabulary*

▶ Did you use a formal, essay-appropriate tone?

▶ Did you use vocabulary familiar to your audience?

5. *Conventions*

▶ Did you follow the rules of grammar usage as well as punctuation, capitalization, and spelling?

On Your Own

TASK 1

Argumentative Essay

Your Assignment

You will read two texts about keeping exotic animals as pets. Then you will write an argumentative essay about whether or not you think people should be allowed to keep exotic animals as pets.

Time Management: Argumentative Task

There are two parts to most formal writing tests. Both parts of the tests are timed, so it's important to use your limited time wisely.

Part 1: Read Sources

35

Preview the Assignment

35 minutes

You will have 35 minutes to read several articles about private citizens keeping exotic animals as pets. You will then answer questions about the texts.

35 minutes! That's not much time.

Preview the questions. This will help you know which information you'll need to find as you read.

How Many?

→ How many pages of reading?

→ How many multiple-choice questions?

→ How many prose constructed-response questions?

How do you plan to use the 35 minutes?

This is a lot to do in a short time.

Estimated time to read:
  "Do You Really Want a Baby Tiger?" [_____] minutes

Estimated time to read:
  "REXANO Proves Politicians and Lobbyists..." [_____] minutes

Estimated time to answer questions? [_____] minutes

Total   **35**   **minutes**

Underline, circle, and take notes as you read. You probably won't have time to reread.

Any concerns?

_____

_____

_____

_____

Part 2: Write the Essay

How much time do you have? Pay attention to the clock!

Plan and Write an Argumentative Essay

85 minutes

You will have 85 minutes to plan, write, revise, and edit your essay.

Your Plan

Before you start to write, decide on your precise claim. Then think about the evidence you will use to support your claim.

How do you plan to use the 85 minutes?

Estimated time for planning the essay?		minutes
Estimated time for writing?		minutes
Estimated time for editing?		minutes
Estimated time for checking spelling, grammar, and punctuation?		minutes
Total	**85**	**minutes**

Be sure to leave enough time for this step.

Notes:

_____

_____

_____

_____

Reread your essay, making sure that the points are clear. Check that there are no spelling or punctuation mistakes.

▶ Your Assignment

> You will read two texts and then write an argumentative essay about whether or not private citizens should be allowed to keep dangerous animals as pets.

Complete the following steps as you compose your essay.

1. Read an article about owning exotic pets.

2. Read an article from a group that supports owners of exotic animals.

3. Answer questions about the sources.

4. Plan, write, and revise your essay.

▶ Part 1 (35 minutes)

As you read the sources, take notes on important facts and details. You may want to refer to your notes while planning and writing your essay.

Do You Really Want a
Baby Tiger?

Second thoughts about owning an exotic pet

by Mia Lewis

NOTES

You know the story: Jenny wants a puppy, but her parents are reluctant to take the plunge. They remind her of the responsibilities that go along with pet ownership: She'll have to take it for a walk, everyday, no matter what; it'll grow up from the cute puppy it is now to a gnarly old dog; there will be messes to clean up, food to buy, and trips to the vet. Jenny says she doesn't mind any of that, and soon Fido is welcomed into the family fold. In no time at all the parents love Fido just as much as Jenny does, and Fido loves them all back. It is a story with a happy ending.

10   But what if Jenny tried to persuade her parents to buy her a fuzzy lion cub she saw advertised, or a baby chimpanzee? If they had any sense, Jenny's parents would tell her "No way" and stick to their guns. Owning an exotic pet is expensive, time consuming, and a huge responsibility. And of course, it can be dangerous. Owning a wild animal is arguably cruel to the animal in a way that owning a domestic animal isn't. Given all these considerations, it's remarkable how many people across the United States decide to become owners of exotic pets.

For some, the allure of owning an exotic pet trumps any
20   drawbacks. After all, it's not your average Joe who owns a python, or a puff adder! A house with a monkey or lion cub in the backyard is going to stand out in the neighborhood. No one will deny that owning an exotic pet is daring and different. But many experts argue that the negatives strongly outweigh the benefits. Here's a look at some of the reasons why owning an exotic animal as a pet is NOT such a good idea.

They all grow up. A cute puppy grows up to be a dog—bigger, but not dangerously so. A lion cub, on the other hand, inevitably turns into, well, a lion. Most people who own exotic pets find them
30   irresistible—and manageable—when they are small. But an adorable cub becomes a powerful adult soon enough. Many exotic animals

are strong enough to be dangerous even without meaning to cause harm. An adult animal is also likely to be aggressive and have more difficult behaviors than a baby one.

Wild animals are wild, even in captivity. A dog is an animal, but it is a *domesticated* one—a species that has evolved over thousands of years to live well with people. Most dogs can be trained with a few puppy obedience classes. Exotic animals are something else entirely. They are wild animals with wild animal instincts, even when born in captivity. A wild animal is never 100 percent predictable. An animal that has behaved one way for many years cannot suddenly change. Domestication is not something that happens in one or two generations: it takes hundreds or thousands of years.

Do you really have the resources? If keeping a dog or cat can be time consuming and costly, that's nothing compared to looking after an adult lion or chimpanzee. It's not just the food and the vet bills, although those can indeed be considerable. You also have to build a sturdy cage or enclosure that is the appropriate size and has the right hiding, resting, climbing, and play spaces to approximate the animal's natural habitat. You will need to be able to devote a large portion of your time to learning about the animal and its needs. Usually only specially trained and qualified individuals working with the backing of a specially equipped facility are fully able to meet the needs of exotic animals. Keep in mind that pet ownership is a lifetime commitment. Jenny's dog may live to be 15, but a chimpanzee can live to be 60 or 65 years old.

Dangers and Diseases. While it is true that even dogs and cats can injure their owners or other people, they do not have the same unpredictable potential for serious or even deadly attacks that many exotic pets do. It's not just big cats, poisonous snakes, and chimpanzees that can be harmful—even smaller exotic pets can cause serious injuries. Exotic pets can also spread diseases to humans. In addition, many exotic pets end up on the loose in the wild. (Owners who find their fully-grown pets unmanageable sometimes release them.) Out on their own, these exotic animals can be a further danger to the public, and even to the environment.

Cruel and Unusual. Many exotic pet owners end up being unable to provide the proper living environment for their fully-grown pets. In order to prevent them from injuring anyone, they may decide to keep them caged. The end result is that far too many of these exotic animals spend almost their entire lives in the "prison" of a small cage. In this kind of environment, they have no opportunity to practice most of their "natural" behaviors.

All in all, Jenny is better off sticking with a "boring" dog or cat. If I were her parents, I'd say yes to the puppy before she got any more "exotic" ideas!

Am I on Track?

Actual Time Spent Reading

REXANO Proves That Politicians and Lobbyists Introducing and Passing Laws Against Exotic Animal Ownership in the Name of 'Public Safety' Use False and Misleading Claims

Private owners of wild and exotic animals in the USA have been coming under ever increasing attacks from animal rights (AR) activists and uninformed legislators to end the private ownership of exotics in the name of "public safety." Many unfair laws have already passed on the federal, state and local levels.

REXANO (Responsible Exotic Animal Ownership), a free web resource designed to give facts-based research material to private owners of exotics to fight unfair legislation, just finished compiling a statistical table proving the legislators passing laws under the guise of
10   public safety used misleading claims.

"In the last 10–16 years, 1.5 people on average gets killed yearly by captive reptile, 1 by captive big cat, 0.81 by captive elephant, 0.125 by captive bear and 0 by captive nonhuman primate," reports Zuzana Kukol, a REXANO co-founder. "As a comparison, 45,000 people die each year in traffic accidents, 47 from lightning and 1,600 by falling down stairs."

"Our statistical analysis of the data disproves the claim that exotic animals in captivity are a threat to public safety. No uninvolved public has ever been killed in the USA since 1990 as a
20   result of a captive big cat, primate, bear, elephant or reptile at large," adds Scott Shoemaker, a REXANO co-founder. "The majority of fatalities are to owners, trainers or people voluntarily visiting the property where the animals are kept."

"If it is illegal for businesses to advertise and sell products using misleading and fraudulent claims, why is it OK for legislators and lobbyists to introduce, gain public support and pass bills using fraudulent claims they can't back up with facts?" asks Kukol. "These bills that waste tax money are appeasing the minority of special interest animal rights groups and a few individuals falling for the
30   claims of imaginary threat at the expense of constitutional freedoms for a majority of Americans. Many animal businesses are regulated out of existence as a result of this deception."

"There are no hard facts and statistics to support the case for these bans, only so-called incident reports compiled by the various AR groups," says Andrew Wyatt, President of NC Association of Reptile Keepers. "These incident reports amount to scary stories about scary animals. Many are unconfirmed, manufactured or ridiculous. Deaths or serious injuries are exceedingly rare. The reality is that you are more likely to contract *E. coli* virus from eating

40 spinach, and die as a result, than die from being attacked by an exotic animal."

"It would be nice if for once the AR fanatics could refrain from exploiting isolated tragic incidents, but they never do. They feed on this kind of hysteria," says Feline Conservation Federation president Lynn Culver. "AR groups use grieving relatives of those harmed by exotic animals as their poster children to help push their agenda of prohibiting exotic animals in society."

"Fear trumps over freedom. Will America be coerced by inflammatory rhetoric from the AR Movement into over reacting to

50 a nonexistent threat by enacting overly intrusive animal bans? I hope not," adds Wyatt.

"Animals are personal property; and we oppose legislation that restricts the private ownership or use of animals, or that inhibits free trade of any animal provided it meets Ohio Department of Agriculture testing and import requirements," adds Polly Britton, Secretary of the Ohio Association of Animal Owners.

"As long as animal welfare and public safety laws are followed, the private ownership of all animals should be protected in the USA," says Shoemaker.

60 "Control the land and the animals, then you control the people," states Kim Bloomer a natural pet care educator, lecturer and host of the online radio show Animal Talk Naturally.

"There is a hidden agenda with regard to all of these laws and it has nothing to do with public safety or concerns for good animal care. Rather, it is about eroding or removing American freedoms, the right to own as many animals as we can provide for."

Current focus of REXANO is to reverse the trend in over regulation.

Am I on Track?

Actual Time Spent Reading

Questions

Answer the following questions. You may refer to your reading notes, and you should cite text evidence in your responses. You will be able to refer to your answers as you write your essay in Part 2.

1 The word *appeasing* is used in the article "REXANO Proves Politicians and Lobbyists..." What is the best synonym for *appeasing*?

    a. shocking

    b. provoking

    c. placating

    d. applauding

2 **Prose Constructed-Response** What are some of the obstacles owners of exotic pets face?

_____

_____

_____

_____

3 **Prose Constructed-Response** Briefly summarize the reasons why REXANO opposes bans on individuals owning exotic pets?

_____

_____

_____

_____

_____

▶ Part 2 (85 minutes)

You now have 85 minutes to review your notes and sources, and to plan, draft, edit, and revise your essay. While you may use your notes and refer to the sources, your essay must represent your original work. You may refer to your responses to Part 1 questions, but you cannot change those answers. Now read your assignment and begin your work.

Your assignment

You have read two texts about keeping exotic animals as pets.

• "Do You Really Want a Baby Tiger?"

• "REXANO Proves Politicians and Lobbyists..."

Consider the information presented about owning exotic pets in each text.

Write an essay that explains your position on owning exotic pets. Remember to use textual evidence to support your claim.

Now begin work on your essay. Manage your time carefully so that you can:

1. plan your essay

2. write your essay

3. revise and edit your final draft

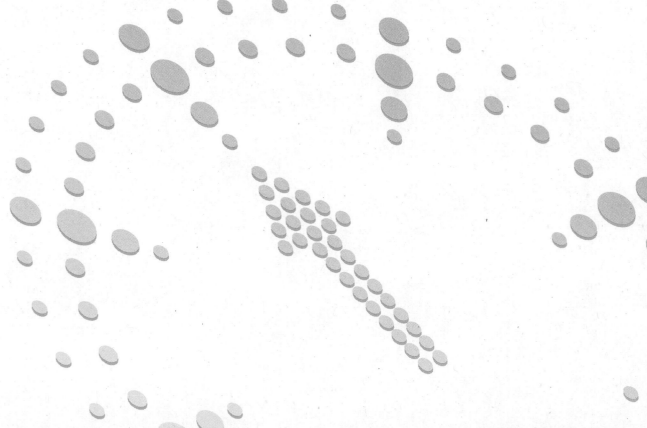

TASK 2

RESEARCH SIMULATION

Informative Essay

Your Assignment

You will read two essays on the importance of communication while hiking. Then you will write an informative essay about why it is important to communicate your whereabouts when going on an outdoor excursion.

Time Management: Informative Task

There are two parts to most formal writing tests. Both parts of the tests are timed, so it's important to use your limited time wisely.

Part 1: Read Sources

Preview the Assignment

35 minutes

You will have 35 minutes to read two selections about hiking outdoors. You will then answer questions about the sources.

> 35 minutes! That's not much time.

How Many?

> Preview the questions. This will help you know which information you'll need to find as you read.

How many pages of reading?

How many multiple-choice questions?

How do you plan to use the 35 minutes?

> Underline, circle, and take notes as you read. You probably won't have time to reread.

Estimated time to read:
   "Miraculous Lost and Found" _____ minutes

> This is a lot to do in a short time.

Estimated time to read:
   "The Most Important Rule" _____ minutes

Estimated time to answer questions? _____ minutes

Total   **35   minutes**

Any concerns?

_____

_____

_____

_____

Part 2: Write the Essay

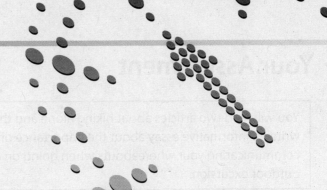

How much time do you have? Pay attention to the clock!

Plan and Write an Informative Essay

85 minutes

You will have 85 minutes to plan, write, revise, and edit your essay.

Your Plan

Before you start writing, decide think about the main idea of your essay. What is the most important point you need to make?

_____

_____

How do you plan to use the 85 minutes?

Estimated time for planning the essay?		minutes
Estimated time for writing?		minutes
Estimated time for editing?		minutes
Estimated time for checking spelling, grammar, punctuation?		minutes
Total	**85**	**minutes**

Be sure to leave enough time for this step.

Notes:

_____

_____

_____

_____

Reread your essay, making sure that the points are clear. Check that there are no spelling or punctuation mistakes.

► Your Assignment

You will read two articles about hiking alone and then write an informative essay about the importance of communicating your whereabouts when going on an outdoor excursion.

Complete the following steps as you plan and compose your essay.

1. Read a news article about a man who became trapped by a boulder when hiking alone.

2. Read an article about rules to follow when hiking.

3. Answer questions about the sources.

4. Plan, write, and revise your essay.

► Part 1 (35 minutes)

As you read the sources, take notes on important facts and details. You may want to refer to your notes while planning and writing your essay.

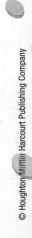

© Houghton Mifflin Harcourt Publishing Company

THE WAYNE COUNTY GAZETTE

Miraculous Lost and Found

by Katherine Leonard,
Staff Writer

Friday, May 2, 2003

NOTES

Aron Ralston, a mountaineer from Aspen, Colorado, lost for over five days in Blue John Canyon, was miraculously found alive yesterday. The experienced climber had been trapped by a big boulder that came loose and pinned his arm against the wall of a narrow canyon that he was descending. Ralston was able to free himself by amputating his arm with a multi-tool pocket knife.

The Meijers, a Dutch family that was hiking in the park, saw Ralston walking aimlessly a few hours after he performed the amputation and immediately gave him food and water, and alerted

10   a rescue team that was already in the area looking for the missing climber.

The authorities are putting together the pieces that form this incredible survival story as more details of Ralston's ordeal surface. It seems that the Colorado climber was mountain-biking in the Canyonlands National Park, when he put down his bike to take a closer look at a very narrow canyon. As he was climbing down, the boulder, with a reported weight of 800 pounds, broke loose and, rolling down, got stuck, pinning Ralston's arm against the wall. Ralston had not told anyone where he was going, or when he

20   expected to return, making a disastrous situation much, much worse.

Slowly consuming the only food he had to eat, two burritos, and taking small sips of his remaining water (about 350 ml), the mountaineer spent the majority of four days waiting for somebody to find him. On his fourth night, he is said to have had an epiphany— amputation was his only way to survive. No one knew he was missing. He would have to rescue himself.

Ralston spent several hours using a dull knife to cut his own arm at the radius. Once free, he rappelled down a 65-foot wall with one hand and started walking the 8 miles that separated him
30 from his car. It was then the Meijer family found him and got help. Ralston was taken to a hospital in Grand Junction, Co., where he remains in critical condition. "He was in pretty rough shape but he communicated with us all the way to the hospital," said the Emery County sheriff Mitch Vetere. "He is obviously a tough guy." Ralston had lost 40 pounds and quite a bit of blood by the time he got to the hospital.

The Most Important Rule

by Jared Myers

As any good adventurist knows, there are a number of common-sense rules to follow when engaging in a successful hike: bring plenty of water, dress appropriately, map out the trail you will be hiking in advance, and be sure to bring along a first aid kit. However, the most important rule of hiking is also one of the most commonly overlooked: Alert a family member or friend to the location of your proposed hike and an estimated time of return.

While any amount of advance planning or familiarity with a particular hiking trail may seem to be an adequate substitute for
10 alerting a friend or loved one, rarely does this planning or familiarity account for an emergency. These unexpected difficulties can come in many forms, including swiftly deteriorating weather conditions, an encounter with dangerous wildlife, or even something as small as a sprained ankle.

For example, in an effort to follow in the footsteps of hiker Aron Ralston, 64-year-old Amos Wayne Richards made an attempt to traverse Utah's Blue John Canyon in September of 2011. However, after falling 10 feet, Richards dislocated his shoulder and shattered his leg. With only two protein bars, an empty water bottle, no family
20 or friends aware of his hiking plans, and no cell phone service with which to contact them, Richards began to drag himself back to his car along the rocky terrain. Four days later, rangers set off to rescue him, tipped off by the discovery of his abandoned campsite and truck. From clues at the campsite and from conversations with Richard's family and friends, rangers figured out where he was likely located and dispatched a helicopter. After using the flash on his camera to catch the attention of the pilot, Amos Wayne Richards was treated for his broken leg and for dehydration at a nearby hospital before being released. The whole ordeal, however, could have been
30 prevented, had he simply informed a friend or family member of his hiking plans and his estimated time of return.

New advancements in technology have made it easier for hikers to plan for unexpected emergencies in advance, without worrying their friends and family unnecessarily. HikerAlert, a web-based service, allows you to enter your hiking itinerary and projected

© Houghton Mifflin Harcourt Publishing Company

return time into its database before your departure. If you fail to respond to a text from the HikerAlert website, checking in with you at your projected return time, a text is sent to your designated emergency contacts entered when the account was created, 40 encouraging them to attempt to contact you.

It's easy to understand why someone may feel it unnecessary to reach out to friends and family before going out on a new adventure. For some, admitting the possibility of danger may make them feel like they appear to be weak or inexperienced. Others may feel that their friends or family may worry too much about them while they are away. However, following this one simple rule may ultimately save your life and ensure that the next hike you go on won't be your last.

Am I on Track?

Actual Time Spent Reading

Questions

Answer the following questions. You may refer to your reading notes, and you should cite text evidence in your responses. Your answers to these questions will be scored. You will be able to refer to your answers as you write your essay in Part 2.

1 What does the word *epiphany* mean as it is used in "Miraculous Lost and Found"?

 a. realization

 b. urge

 c. decision

 d. reluctance

2 Which word or phrase best help the reader understand the meaning of *epiphany*?

 a. "'He was in pretty rough shape but he communicated . . .'" (lines 32–33)

 b. "'. . . he rappelled down a 65-foot wall . . .'" (line 28)

 c. ". . . amputation was his only way to survive." (line 25)

 d. "aimlessly" (line 8)

3 Which of the following sentences best states an accurate claim one could make after reading these selections?

 a. Amos Wayne Richards's accident was unrelated to Ralston's accident.

 b. The Meijers family found Ralston because they were aware of his location.

 c. Aron Ralston knew the area was dangerous because many people had been injured by boulders there.

 d. Technology can be an important asset for hikers.

4 Which piece of evidence best supports your answer to Question 3?

 a. ". . . a text is sent to your designated emergency contacts entered when the account was created . . ." (Source 2, lines 38–39)

 b. ". . . attempt to traverse Utah's Blue John Canyon . . ." (Source 2, lines 16–17)

 c. "Once free, he rappelled down a 65-foot wall with one hand . . ." (Source 1, lines 28–29)

 d. "The experienced climber had been trapped by a big boulder that came loose and pinned his arm against the wall of a narrow canyon that he was descending." (Source 1, lines 3–5)

▶ Part 2 (85 minutes)

You have 85 minutes to review your notes and sources, and to plan, draft, edit, and revise your essay. While you may use your notes and refer to the sources, your work must represent your original work. You may refer to your responses to Part 1 questions, but you cannot change those answers. Now read your assignment and begin your work.

Your assignment

You have read two texts about hiking alone.

• "Miraculous Lost and Found"

• "The Most Important Rule"

Consider the information presented about the dangers of hiking alone.

Write an essay that explains why it is important to communicate your destination when hiking alone. Remeber to use textual evidence to support your claim.

Now begin work on your essay. Manage your time carefully so that you can:

1. plan your essay

2. write your essay

3. revise and edit your final draft

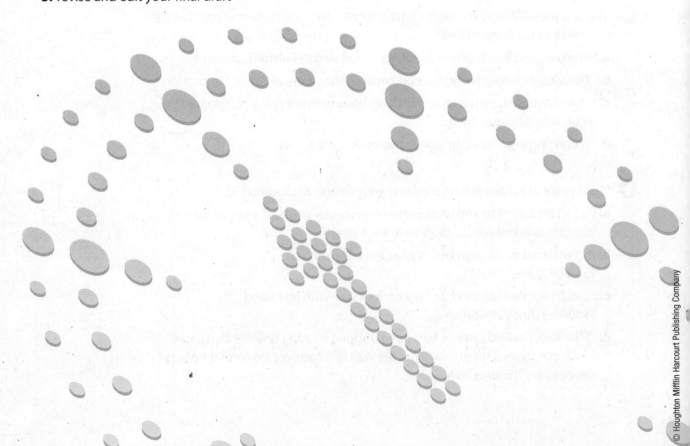

TASK 3

Literary Analysis

Your Assignment

You will write a literary analysis comparing how Helen of Troy is portrayed in Edgar Allan Poe's "To Helen" and H. D.'s "Helen."

Time Management: Literary Analysis Task

Most formal writing tests are made up of two parts. Both parts of the tests are timed, so it's important to use your limited time wisely.

Part 1: Read Sources

Preview the Assignment

35 minutes

You will have 35 minutes to read two poems to discover how the same subject, Helen of Troy, is treated differently in the two texts. You will then answer questions about each text.

35 minutes! That's not much time.

How Many?

Preview the questions. This will help you know which information you'll need to find as you read.

How many pages of reading?

How many multiple-choice questions?

How many prose constructed-response questions?

How do you plan to use the 35 minutes?

This is a lot to do in a short time.

Estimated time to read:
   "To Helen" _____ minutes

Estimated time to read:
   "Helen" _____ minutes

Estimated time to answer questions? _____ minutes

Total **35** **minutes**

Underline, circle, and take notes as you read. You probably won't have time to reread.

Any concerns?

_____

_____

_____

_____

Part 2: Write the Analysis

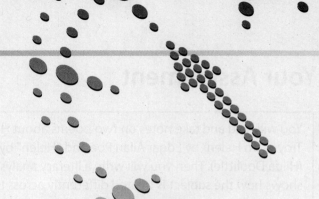

How much time do you have? Pay attention to the clock!

Plan and Write a Literary Analysis

→ 85 minutes

You will have 85 minutes to plan, write, revise, and edit your literary analysis.

Your Plan

Before you start writing, decide how you will organize your literary analysis:

Point-by-Point? ☐   Subject-by-Subject? ☐

How do you plan to use the 85 minutes?

Estimated time for planning the essay? ☐ minutes

Estimated time for writing? ☐ minutes

Estimated time for editing? ☐ minutes

Estimated time for checking spelling, grammar, punctuation? ☐ minutes

Total **85** **minutes**

Be sure to leave enough time for this step.

Notes:

_____

_____

_____

_____

Reread your essay, making sure that the points are clear. Check that there are no spelling or punctuation mistakes.

▶ Your Assignment

> You will read and take notes on two poems about Helen of Troy—"To Helen" by Edgar Allan Poe and "Helen" by H. D. (Hilda Doolittle). Then you will write a literary analysis that shows how the subject is treated differently across the two texts.

Complete the following steps as you plan and compose your essay.

1. Read the poem "To Helen" by Edgar Allan Poe.

2. Read the poem "Helen" by H. D.

3. Answer questions about the sources.

4. Plan, write, and revise your essay.

▶ Part 1 (35 minutes)

As you read the sources, take notes on important facts and details. You may want to refer to your notes while planning and writing your essay.

To Helen

by Edgar Allan Poe

Helen, thy beauty is to me
    Like those Nicéan barks of yore,
That gently, o'er a perfumed sea,
    The weary, way-worn wanderer bore
5   To his own native shore.°

On desperate seas long wont to roam,
    Thy hyacinth hair, thy classic face,
Thy Naiad° airs have brought me home
    To the glory that was Greece,
10   And the grandeur that was Rome.

Lo! in yon brilliant window-niche
    How statuelike I see thee stand,
The agate lamp within thy hand!
    Ah, Psyche,° from the regions which
15   Are Holy Land!

---

5. **Nicéan . . . shore:** Nicea was a Greek colony; the wanderer referred to is Odysseus.
8. **Naiad:** nymphlike.
14. **Psyche:** mortal woman whose great beauty captivated Cupid, the god of Love.

NOTES

Am I on Track?

Actual Time Spent Reading

Helen

by H. D.

All Greece hates
the still eyes in the white face,
the luster as of olives
where she stands,
5   and the white hands.

All Greece reviles
the wan face when she smiles,
hating it deeper still
when it grows wan and white,
10   remembering past enchantments
    and past ills.

Greece sees unmoved,
God's daughter,° born of love,
the beauty of cool feet
15   and slenderest knees,
could love indeed the maid,
only if she were laid,
white ash amid funereal cypresses.

---

13. God's daughter: Helen was a daughter of Zeus, the king of the gods. She was conceived when Zeus (in the form of a swan) seduced the mortal Leda.

Am I on Track?

Actual Time Spent Reading

Questions

Answer the following questions. You may refer to your reading notes, and you should cite text evidence in your responses. Your answers to these questions will be scored. You bill be able to refer to your answers as you write your essay in Part 2.

1 What does the word *barks* mean in these lines from the poem "To Helen"?

> "Helen, thy beauty is to me
>> Like those Nicéan barks of yore,
> That gently, o'er a perfumed sea,
>> The weary, way-worn wanderer bore
>> To his own native shore."
>
> (lines 1–5)

   a. harsh sounds

   b. sailors

   c. outer covering of trees

   d. ships

2 Which word (or phrase) from "To Helen" in Question 1 best helps you understand the meaning of *barks*?

   a. "Nicéan"

   b. "way-worn wanderer"

   c. "o'er a perfumed sea"

   d. "gently"

3 Which of the following sentences best states an important difference between the two poems concerning their depiction of Helen of Troy?

   a. In contrast to Poe's poem, H. D.'s poem celebrates Helen for her classic beauty.

   b. The speaker in Poe's poem compares Helen to a "weary, way-worn wanderer," whereas in H. D.'s poem the speaker compares her to a lifeless statue.

   c. In Poe's poem, Helen is worshiped for her beauty, whereas in H. D.'s poem, her face is detested by the Greeks.

   d. Although both poets draw attention to Helen's face, Poe treats it as an example of classic beauty, whereas H. D. depicts it as fierce and savage.

4 Select two pieces of evidence from the poem "To Helen" by Edgar Allan Poe and two pieces of evidence from the poem "Helen" by H. D. that support the answer to Question 3.

    a. "Helen, thy beauty is to me / Like those Nicéan barks of yore . . . " ("To Helen," lines 1–2)

    b. "That gently, o'er a perfumed sea, / The weary, way-worn wanderer bore . . . " ("To Helen," lines 3–4)

    c. "Thy hyacinth hair, thy classic face, / Thy Naiad airs have brought me home . . . " ("To Helen," lines 7–8)

    d. "Lo! in yon brilliant window-niche / How statuelike I see thee stand . . . " ("To Helen," lines 11–12)

    e. "All Greece hates / the still eyes in the white face . . . " ("Helen," lines 1–2)

    f. "All Greece reviles / the wan face when she smiles . . . " ("Helen," lines 6–7)

    g. "God's daughter, born of love . . . " ("Helen," line 13)

    h. "the beauty of cool feet / and slenderest knees . . . " ("Helen," lines 14–15)

5 **Prose Constructed-Response** According to H. D., what do the people of Greece think of Helen? Cite specific evidence from the text in your response.

© Houghton Mifflin Harcourt Publishing Company

► Part 2 (85 minutes)

You will have 85 minutes to review your notes and sources, and to plan, draft, edit, and revise your essay. While you may use your notes and refer to the sources, your essay must represent your original work. You may refer to your responses to Part 1, but you cannot changes those answers. Now read your assignment and begin your work.

Your assignment

You have read two poems about Helen of Troy.

- "To Helen" by Edgar Allan Poe

- "Helen" by H. D.

Write a literary analysis essay that compares and contrasts the way Helen is treated in these two poems.

1. plan your essay

2. write your essay

3. revise and edit your final draft

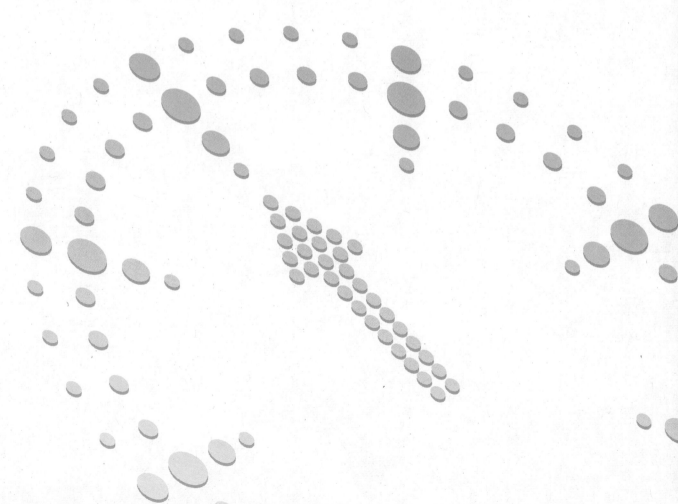

Acknowledgments

"Helen" from *Collected Poems 1912–1944* by H.D. Text copyright © 1982 by the Estate of Hilda Doolittle. Reprinted by permission of New Directions Publishing Corporation and Carcanet.

"REXANO Proves Politicians and Lobbyists Introducing and Passing Laws Against Exotic Animal Ownership in the Name of 'Public Safety' Use False and Misleading Claims" from *PRWeb,* March 17, 2007, www.prweb.com. Text copyright © 2007 by Rexano. Reprinted by permission of Rexano.

"Social Media, Pretend Friends, and the Lie of False Intimacy" by Jay Baer from *Convince & Convert,* www.convinceandconvert.com. Text copyright © 2008-2013 by Convince & Convert, LLC. Reprinted by permission of Convince & Convert, LLC.

"Spring is like a perhaps hand" from *Complete Poems: 1904–1962* by E. E. Cummings. Text copyright © 1923, 1925, 1951, 1953, 1991 by the Trustees for the E. E. Cummings Trust. Text copyright © 1976 by George James Firmage. Reprinted by permission of Liveright Publishing Corporation.

"Study: The Internet Helps You Make More Friends, Be More Social" by Graeme McMillan from *Time,* June 16, 2011, www.techland.time.com. Text copyright © 2011 by Time, Inc. Reprinted by permission of Time, Inc.